music of the mind

darryl reanney

music of the mind

an adventure into consciousness

SOUVENIR PRESS

First published in Australia by
Hill of Content Publishing, Melbourne

First British edition published 1995 by
Souvenir Press Ltd,
43 Great Russell Street, London WC1B 3PA
and simultaneously in Canada

ISBN 0 285 63288 4

Printed and bound in Great Britain by
Biddles Ltd, Guildford and King's Lynn

The author wishes to thank Professor Kenneth Ring of the
University of Connecticut for his helpful contributions to
the evolution of this book and Dr John Jenkin of La Trobe
University for reviewing the book from the perspective of a
physicist. He is also grateful to Vanda Jackson for
introducing him to the poetry of Kathleen Raine.

The circumstances of this book are unusual. Between closure
of the text editing, and publication, Darryl Reanney was
stricken with acute myeloid leukaemia. His perception on
receipt of the page proofs, just prior to publication, was
that the book was too arrogant and in places the science was
pushed unacceptably too far. He wanted the text
withdrawn. A group of close friends insisted however that
the book had left him already, a child of time and space
probing beyond itself and with the facts of its birth yielding
to it a special power.

to Elisabeth

Contents

author's preface v

introduction   another way of knowing 1

1 the dream that woke 17

2 the image of eternity 30

3 the ticking of the clock 37

4 a tale of two flowers 44

5 falling into time 53

6 thinking the thought 62

7 realities we do not see 71

8 knowing the magic key 82

9 the dark portal 95

10 shards of truth 115

11 the cosmic balance 131

12 a beauty too terrible to see 144

13 phase transition 161

references 173

bibliography 181

When I was young I fell in love with a piece of music by Don McLean called 'American Pie', with one stanza in particular:

I went down to the sacred store
where I heard the music years before
but the man there said the music wouldn't play.
And in the streets the children screamed,
the lovers cried and the poets dreamed.
But not a word was spoken
the church bells all were broken . . .[1]

Why did this touch a raw nerve in me? The answer lies less in the rhythm of the music than in the message of the lyric. We live in a society which is undergoing a profound crisis of meaning. For most of us the music *has* stopped, the church bells *are* all broken and we do not know where to look to find a convincing reason for our existence. In a quite profound sense, we have lost our way. Why?

My explanation is simple: I believe society is sick, at least in part, because we have lost the 'story' that bound us together. It is part of our human necessity that we need to be animated by some deep sense of common purpose, of shared meaning, if our lives are not to become pointless irrelevancies. Without an underpinning foundation of explanatory story we find it hard to experience enthusiasm in the true sense of its original meaning—being *en* (in) *theos* (God).

Paradoxically, however, the agent that destroyed the old sense of shared myth may itself be the midwife that gives birth to the new. A revelatory story is emerging from modern science, a story which no longer sees human beings as accidental side issues in a mechanical universe but as co-creative participants in an adventure-driven mystery. At the centre of this evolving story is the ethic of interconnectedness; science is now validating the central insight of the sacred tradition, 'all is one', showing that the part has no meaning outside the whole, that to explain anything you have to explain everything.

For society the problem is that science is changing much faster than the attitudes it gave rise to. While the machine paradigm fades from science itself, it lingers stubbornly in the social and intellectual conventions that still look to science for their endorsement. Thus the human body is still spoken of in the language of mechanism, psychiatric treatment still relies heavily on palliatives and tranquillisers, and we deny the role of touch—the most reassuring and healing of all human interactions—in the very areas that we need it most. We do all these things because we have forgotten what our ancestors understood at a deep level, that no society can be whole while any one of its member parts is damaged; any music ceases to be harmonic if a single note is off-key.

This has been part of the 'dark side' of our scientific culture. In its relentless pursuit of objectivity it appealed to the mind but not the heart; by elevating logic to supreme status it relegated feeling to the category of a distraction. So began that unnatural 'split' in the Western psyche that has been a root cause of our cultural pathology; thus, long ago, we became the divided beings we still are.

The modern crisis of meaning has a very personal dimension for me. When I was eighteen my mother had a stroke and was rushed to hospital, unconscious. Several weeks later she died, in the presence of my father but the absence of me, her son, because the hospital rules of that time forbade the attendance of juniors at a death watch. Two months later I had my first attack of what was later diagnosed as agoraphobia. Unknown to most GPs in the 1950s, this condition was inevitably confused with 'nervous breakdown' and the next ten years of my life were spent in a contracted world in which fear, my ever-present companion, shadowed every step I took outside the familiar sanctuary of my bedroom. It is a situation well-known to sufferers from this rare condition but incomprehensible to that mythical beast, 'the average person'. Thus I learned the hard way what it means to be different.

Decades after the event I commit this to paper, not to arouse sympathy but to make a point; my university studies, just begun when my mother died, became under the impetus of her death the only thing that kept me sane. What might, under other circumstances, have been an intellectual game became for me a grim issue of simple survival; in order to keep going I had to know whether life had a purpose.

So the search for meaning has been the driving force of my life across the three decades that have gone by since that night the normal world ended for me. In terms of knowedge it has led me from the humanities to the sciences, from the study of Shakespeare to the study of subatomic structure. In terms of travel it has led me from the green haven of my New Zealand origins to the crowded hustle of most of the world's great cities. And to many other places. Looking back at that search down the arches of the years I have to say that it has not played me false. From the wreckage of those ruined yesterdays has come an unquenchable optimism about the tomorrow of our species. One of my deepest convictions, and the impetus for this book, is that the anxiety-ridden convulsions of our time are only the growing pains of consciousness as it struggles to free itself from the littleness of self.

Throughout my life I have found that the best way to understand something is to write it down in my own words. This book is a record of my attempt to answer the bruising questions that trouble this generation as they have troubled all that went before it: 'Who am I? Where did I come from? What happens when I die? Is there a God?'. In the particular form in which I have written it this book is the record of one individual's journey. But in a more general sense it is the journey we all make as we struggle to find that familiar stranger—the person we have the capacity to become.

Some time ago I wrote of this struggle:

> If we want to see the universe as consciousness knows it we should stop thinking of it as a machine or a process or a system and start thinking of it as a *song*.[2]

Encrypted in that statement was the seed of a liberating insight. This book represents the unhusking of that seed. What follows is, I hope, not offered in arrogance but in the spirit of John Greenleaf Whittier's poem:

> Let the thick curtain fall
> I better know than all
> How little I have gained;
> How vast the unattained.

> Others shall sing the song,
> Others shall right the wrong,—
> Finish what I begin,
> And all I fail of win.[3]

Time past and time future
Allow but a little consciousness.
To be conscious is not to be in time.

T.S. ELIOT

another way of
knowing

To leave the comfort zone we now inhabit, we have to learn a new way of seeing. Or an old way we have forgotten how to use.

To get into this let me try to awaken in you a sense of the *strangeness* of things. Straight away there is resistance. There is a strong temptation to say, 'Things are not strange. I'm here, my house is here. The paper arrived this morning, as usual; it's all safe and familiar'. But here is precisely my jump-off point. It's familiar only because of habituation, because who we are and what we see has been patterned and reinforced by layers of experience, repeated across days, months, years. This process of repetitive conditioning does not take us closer to truth; it removes us from truth, dulling perception in the precise measure that it strengthens habit.

What we have lost, to our enormous detriment, is the freshness of a child's mind. Pre-industrial societies understood this. The Chinese philosopher Mencius said, 'The whole purpose of education is to recapture the mind of a child'; Jesus said, 'Except you become as little children you shall not enter the kingdom of heaven'.

What is the special gift of childhood that is destroyed by

the act of growing up? Simply, it is our capacity to wonder. When you were a child did you ever steal into a paddock just before dawn, when the first chill flush of light was washing across the sky, when the earth was hushed and the creatures of the earth still sleeping? Remember that moment of miracle when the horizontal rays of the just-risen sun turned the necklaces of dewdrops on spiderwebs in the grass into radiant circlets of diamonds? Remember that aching sense of abundant beauty, when the earth was so magnificent it hurt?

> Across the long lapse of lost years,
> and squandered certainties
> that dawn is still in me
> I can see the glitter-crystals looped on spiderwebs
> I can hear the expectant silence
> I can taste the eager freshness of that vanished air
> even now that I am old.

In this book I am going to ask you to come with me on a journey of discovery, back into that forgotten time of the otherness of things. How will we do this? It isn't easy. We have to dig deep, below the crusty detritus of routine; we have to unlearn prejudice, unremember ourselves, go back to the source, seeing the world as it is, not as we think it is.

> I am face to face with something that is not myself, or of my
> imagining, something that belongs to another order of being,
> which I come out of the depths of myself to meet as at the surface
> of a glass. Is it the child in me? Which child? Where does he come
> from? Who is he?[4]

On the journey of exploration this book tracks we will use the lens of that eclipsed simplicity. To take the opening step look at Figure 1. This shows the evolutionary sequence according to our experience:

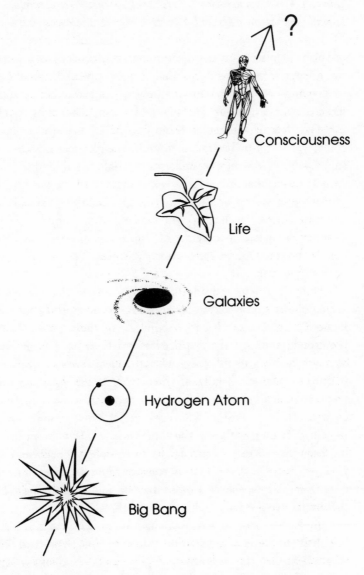

Figure 1 A schematic representation of the evolutionary sequence, according to modern science

3

*Big Bang→formless clouds of hydrogen and helium gas→proto
galaxies→first generation stars and planets→supernovae→
second generation stars and planets→life→consciousness.*

Spend a minute or two examining this, processing it with
the mental software you are used to using. Now I invite you
to try and see it differently, allowing—not denying— your
sense of wonder. What does Figure 1 mean, what does it tell
us? That from hydrogen, the simplest of all the atoms, have
come symphony orchestras, diamonds, the glimmer of dew on
spiderwebs at dawn, the underwater flight of dolphins, the
colours inside abalone shells, Voyager spacecraft, fractal images
on computer screens and the laser light of cognitive awareness.
This is not a mechanical progression from simplicity to
complexity; it is a creative act of stupendous proportions. We
are the products of this evolutionary process. We are also its
heirs and its trustees.

I want to try to add another layer of meaning to this, by
asking you to go on a kind of guided meditation into yourself.
Figure 2 shows a graphic representation of the simplest state,
the ground state, of the hydrogen atom. Imagine the universe
as it was shortly after its genesis when this elementary structure—
hydrogen—was essentially all there was (I am ignoring the
presence of helium since helium, an inert gas, plays a limited
creative role in the evolution of the universe). Now jump forward
to yourself, understanding that the work of 15 billion years
has been needed to bridge that gap in complexity between the
seed you were and the person you are. This is an exercise I
do for myself whenever I want to put my consciousness in
the proper perspective of where it came from.

I emphasise that this way of seeing is no retreat into mawkish
romanticism. It is just as factual, just as much the truth of
what science says as anything we might read in textbooks which
are usually written using a more limiting software, based on
what one could almost call 'scientific fundamentalism'. I believe

that if we allow ourselves to see in this more revelatory way we are seeing more honestly; we are relinquishing the lens of so-called objectivity, which bleeds this spectacle of colour by seeing it only in intellectual terms; we are allowing ourselves to know the reality of grandeur when grandeur so patently exists.

In viewing the message of science this way we are tapping into what I like to call *another way of knowing*. In my view, the basic flaw of almost all science presentation is its dependence on logic. At first sight it seems heresy to question the role of logic since deductive reasoning has been elevated to something near divine status by the sociology of our time. Yet logic is not the only way we know the world and not necessarily the best. Consider T.S. Eliot's famous lines from 'Little Gidding':

> We shall not cease from exploration
> and the end of all our exploring
> will be to arrive where we started
> and know the place for the first time.[5]

I have found that most people react to this poem in a special way; they recognise something in it, they sense *that* it is true without being able to see *why* it is true. This, I submit, is because great poetry reaches into a well of understanding that logic cannot tap.

This different way of knowing finds its most perfect expression in *paradox*. A simple example of paradox is the folk-saying: *The best way to learn something is to teach it.* This aphorism contains the basic elements of paradox; its two hinge elements, *learn* and *teach*, are symmetrically opposed in meaning yet, by grace of this very opposition, the statement conveys a basic truth in a highly compact form. But it is not only information-dense; it has genuine depth.

Another example of paradox is encoded in the sacred insight: *He who loses his life shall find it.* Here again we have

Figure 2 The cosmos grows from simplicity into sentience. The fuzzy sphere above is a representation of the simplest state of the simplest atom (hydrogen); the face opposite is one of the products of that primordial hydrogen, after 15 billion years of evolution.

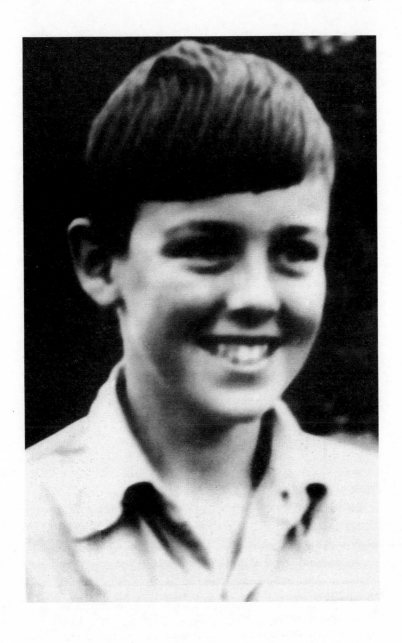

symmetrically opposed elements, *loss* and *discovery*, in this case united in a key statement that accesses a very deep level of meaning. This sacred saying highlights a critical aspect of paradox; either it is understood immediately in the original sense of 'without mediation' (explanation) or not understood at all. Which means, simply, that the mind of the reader (listener) must be *ready* to receive the message; it must have been adequately prepared by prior experience, otherwise there will be no music, only noise. If one thinks of the mind in terms of a receiving instrument like a radio one can say that the set must be *tuned to the right frequency* to access the meaning.

A poem built on paradox is 'Creation of Ea':

Only in silence the word,
only in dark the light,
only in dying life:
bright the hawk's flight
on the empty sky.[6]

The Nazarene Jesus highlights the radical importance of paradox in the evolution of consciousness when he says, using (I believe) the word 'Kingdom' with the exact sense of the Buddhist 'state of enlightenment':

When you make the two one, and
when you make the inner as the outer
and the outer as the inner
and the above
as the below, and when
you make the male and the female into a single one
then shall you enter the Kingdom.[7]

Again, these lines rouse feelings of resonance in us, yet not only are they illogical, their opposing propositions are, in terms of logic, contradictory.

8

This example demonstrates the special virtue of paradoxes; they 'work' because they *reconcile opposites*. This implies that a paradox must necessarily transcend logic to blend in understanding items of awareness that reason automatically cancels out. Or to put the same message a different way, a paradox must draw on a quality of understanding other than logic since its essence is the contradiction of logic. The difference may be partly due to the characteristically holistic quality of 'right-brain' insight as opposed to the typically linear quality of 'left-brain' logic but to regard this simple separation of function as an explanation is to trivialise the meaning the word 'explain'.

In the case of Jesus' saying, the script reads like a code. And there is a 'code-breaker'—the words 'when you make the male and the female into a single one'. Every adult can relate to this, understanding that man and woman become one in the act of love. So the intuitive implication is that enlightenment is reached when all opposites are joined in one. This appears to have been the belief of Neils Bohr, founding father of the branch of science called quantum mechanics. Asked to contribute a 'quote for posterity' on a blackboard reserved for such memorabilia at Moscow University, he wrote *Contraria non contradictoria sed complementa sunt* (Opposites are not contradictory but complementary).

I can best sum up the point of paradoxes in the allegorical language in which they are usually cast. *Things which seem opposite in ignorance are reconciled in knowing.* Each half of a paradoxical contradiction is not the enemy but the brother of its partner; each half is necessary for the whole, each fits the other, just as lock and key fit together to open the door of understanding.

In more scientific language I can say that the essence of paradox is a *symmetry which is broken*. The symmetry comes from the equality between the two halves of the paradoxical equation—learn/teach; lose/find; silence/word; inner/outer.

The breaking comes from their opposition. The allegory of a balance which is broken to create meaning is a leitmotif of this text.

It is important to stress just how different this way of 'seeing' is from the way of scientific procedure. Science's search for truth requires it to excise the very contradictions on which paradoxes rest. If it were possible to reduce a paradox to a mathematical proposition the resulting statement would tend to falsify itself. This self-defeating limitation is built into the structure of logic itself.

We can glean some feeling for the reason behind this by considering a simple self-referential conundrum quoted by Paul Davies:

SOCRATES   What Plato is about to say is false.
PLATO   Socrates has spoken truly.[8]

This example contains the contradictory elements of a paradox without a paradox's depth. It is not a true paradox because our minds do not need to reconcile its opposing elements on the same deep level and in the same deep way as they do with the saying, 'He who loses his life shall find it'. But while it does not 'touch' us, it does serve to illustrate the kinds of problem that arise from any attempt to build a self-consistent model of the world on purely logical principles. On the level of mere logic, opposing propositions remain contradictory and self-negating; they do not access the deep reaches of our knowing because they cannot. Indeed, a general proof called 'Goedel's theorem' shows that, ultimately, no self-consistent mathematical structure can ever be constructed which explains and encompasses the total richness of the world's truth. There will always be truth that lies beyond.

Much of this limitation of logic has to do with its literalness. Carl Sagan quotes the example of a language computer which, when asked to translate the folk-saying 'Out of sight, out of mind', came back with the answer 'Invisible idiot'.[9] One may be tempted to infer that this particular instance of literal-mindedness was a function of the limited sophistication of the computer, that a better computer might be able to decode the saying correctly. This may be true in many cases but in the widest context I am in complete agreement with scientists like Roger Penrose who believe that the mechanism of consciousness is at root non-algorithmic, which means that consciousness cannot be reduced to purely computational principles, although it can—and does—use computation to arrive at logical conclusions about the way things work.[10]

My belief is simply this: paradoxes tap directly into the non-algorithmic depth of knowing. As do poetry and music. The use of non-algorithmic knowing does not mean that one has to abandon science. Just the reverse. Philosopher of science Thomas Kuhn has pointed out that almost all the great advances in science have come about not from logic or reason but from 'Eureka' moments—flashes of insight that are at root indistinguishable from the moments of *creative inspiration* that fire music, literature or art.[11] After the instantaneous synthesis of a deep insight the crafting of a detailed scientific theory is only a sophisticated 'mopping up' operation. Logic is thus the *tool* of insight, not its guide.

If scientific and artistic insights both stem from non-algorithmic consciousness then those aesthetic qualities that cluster round the word 'beautiful' should have some guiding role in our quest for truth. Many scientists now believe this. Listen to the physicist David Bohm speaking in an interview conducted not long before his death in 1992:

. . . Bohm expected that science and art would someday merge. 'This division of art and science is temporary,' he said. 'It didn't exist in the past, and there's no reason why it should go on in the future.' Just as art consists not simply of works of art but of an 'attitude, the artistic spirit', so does science consist not in the accumulation of knowledge but in the creation of fresh modes of perception.[12]

In like vein, the French mathematician Poincaré:

The most useful combinations are precisely the most beautiful. I mean those best able to charm this special sensibility that all mathematicians know . . . Among great numbers of combinations blindly formed by the subliminal self, almost all are without interest and without utility, but for just that reason they are also without effect upon the aesthetic sensibility. Consciousness will never know them.[13]

The history of science is rich in examples. When James Clerk Maxwell was wrestling with the equations that govern electricity and magnetism (previously thought to be separate forces) he arrived at two equations which seemed to hold the answer. But the equations didn't 'look right', they lacked elegance. So for purely aesthetic reasons Maxwell added an extra term, to restore symmetry. And behold, electricity and magnetism were revealed as complementary aspects of the same force.

Another example comes from my own speciality, molecular biology. In 1953, J.D. Watson and Francis Crick discovered that the genetic molecule, DNA, had a repetitive double helical structure somewhat like the intercoiled snake motif that symbolises the Yoga concept of kundalini. This was striking because it showed that no matter how different the species of creature, be it a butterfly or an aardvark or an elephant, the molecules in whose script the book of life was written had the same reiterative format. The music of life was encrypted in the symmetry of a crystal. Writing to his friend about the double helical structure, Watson made the telltale comment: 'It's too pretty not to be true'. So, here again, the truth of a scientific insight was being judged—by one of its discoverers—in terms of *aesthetic* criteria.

This process tends to reach its apogee in modern physics. The physicist Paul Dirac once said, 'A theory with mathematical beauty is more likely to be correct than an ugly one that fits some experiments'. Einstein also put great faith in the artistry of mathematical symbolism. Indeed, asked what he would do if the Special Theory of Relativity were proved wrong, Einstein replied, 'Then I should be sorry for the Good Lord; the theory is right'. This innocent blasphemy highlights the sense of intuitive certainty that usually accompanies deep insight.

I can combine all this as follows: aesthetic resonances typify non-algorithmic knowing, and non-algorithmic knowing is responsible for almost all the insights that drive the key advances in science, literature and music. If one now asks 'Why this mysterious concordance between aesthetic judgement and the inner structure of reality?' I would answer, simply, that the universe is most truly understood when it is viewed, not a machine or a process but as *an evolving work of art*.

My book lives out the message of this, its opening chapter. It is an attempt to reconcile what many people still see as opposites but which I see as complementary—the seemingly divergent pathways tracked by science on the one hand and the sacred traditions on the other. It is written in the spirit of my favourite proverb, a Buddhist saying which, while not itself a paradox, provides a perfect metaphor of the lucid symmetry from which a paradox takes its power:

> The soul of humanity is like a bird with two wings; one wing is wisdom, the other compassion; the bird will only fly if both wings are in perfect balance.

What is different about this book is the way it attempts to access the truths that science has uncovered by abandoning the tools that science has used, tapping instead into this other way of knowing. Thus the book deals with the topics it treats in terms of *metaphors*, making as much use of parable and poetry as possible and using paradox as a structuring theme of the text. This may cause problems for those trained in or familiar with the scientific method, so let me caution at the beginning that *a metaphor is not a model*. My whole point is that the aesthetic approach is not demonstrable in the self-confirming sense that science has led us to demand of logical 'proof'. Everything I have written in *Music of the Mind* is consistent with the general body of scientific knowledge as I understand it but, because it attempts to reach a deeper level of knowing than that mapped out by the 'theorem method' of step-by-step reasoning, its revelations may not be fully explicable in terms of the current scientific mindset.

When I was at university there was a joke that information went from the sheet of paper in front of the lecturer to the sheet of paper in front of the student without passing through the mind of either. This wisecrack highlights a basic issue inherent in any attempt to transmit knowing; a book is only one half of an equation of understanding. The preparedness of your mind is the other. If you are ready to hear then I hope what this books says will be meaningful for you in terms of your life's journey. If you are ready there will be a *resonance* between my mind and yours. This means that you will understand much more than the words themselves because you will be able to access the ideas they reflect without mediation. Or, to put it another way, knowing that there are two halves to this equation of understanding—my mind and yours—I will present my ideas as though I were in the room with you, engaging you in a two-way interaction in which my thoughts 'send' while yours 'receive'.

To begin I would like to use a parable which seems appropriate. My hope is that this book will be for you what it has been for me—a voyage of self-discovery. The essence of a voyage is that *the landscape is always changing*. This affects the way we 'understand' in an important way. Each time we learn something important, something we did not know before, we change; the person that asks question B is not the person who asks question A.

I would like you to imagine a Christmas present, a box that is wrapped in many layers of transparent paper, each a different colour. The unopened present that is the composite of all the colours seems murky, dark, almost black. This is where we stand now, at the beginning of our exploration. As we approach each issue this book deals with, it will be like peeling off a single layer of wrapping. *It is only when the layer comes off that you see its true colour* and it is only when its coverings are removed that you start to see the true character of the box that is *the object of our search*. So that when finally we get to the centre, the box we originally thought was black will have become green, then blue, then red, then gold. For here is a necessary insight: at the level of comprehension at which it is usually pitched, *truth is relative to the mindset you bring to it*.

The first 'layer' to be unwrapped is the Genesis question, 'Where did I come from?'. Then we look at time in terms of its two (apparently) contradictory aspects, being and becoming. Next we unwrap the many layers of meaning that cluster round the issue of quantum mechanics as we investigate the vexed issue of the relationship between subject and object, between the world 'out there' and the world 'in here'. This leads to a quantum mechanical interpretation of consciousness, which is the hinge on which the whole book hangs. In terms of this interpretation, it is not only possible for consciousness to survive death; rather, the unbroken continuity of consciousness reveals itself as a logical and utterly inevitable consequence of the way the world is woven. The last section of the book looks at issues of ultimate meaning, not as abstract ideas in some musty text, but as the source of the passion that drives our lives.

So let us start to track this spoor that leads us in search of ourselves. In the spirit of David Malouf's haunting question:

> What else should our lives be then, but a continuous series of beginnings, of painful steppings out, pushing off from the edges of consciousness into the mystery of what we have not yet become?[14]

Chapter 1

the dream that woke

In the beginning . . .

Even now the words are evocative of mystery. And even now there is an absolute conceptual barrier to their understanding. Science says the universe 'began' in what it calls, in its own mythic language, a quantum fluctuation. But when we ask 'What is this?' we run headlong into a situation where language falters on the brink of breakdown. I could speak of a point that is not a place and a moment that is not a time, of a micro-bubble of nothing, but the words would distort the very phenomenon they were seeking to define. At the barrier between existence and non-existence we approach a place where truth can only be glimpsed in paradox: *an emptiness that yet is full.*

The Judeo-Christian tradition says 'Thou shalt not look upon the face of God and live'. There is a sense in which those words belong here. Behind the barrier of the absolute beginning may be the bland void of utter nothingness or there may be *a beauty too terrible to look upon.* The Genesis event is hidden from us by a veil which our minds, as they are presently constructed, cannot penetrate. A mystery. All we can say is

17

that, somehow, out of that mystery there exploded a fireball of unimaginable power. And this we can say confidently: all that was, all that is and all that shall be, was contained in that fireball.

Those words slide so easily from the pen but what writer in the wildest moment of his most unfettered dream, at the outermost limit of the most audacious act of an enraptured imagination could have conceived of a genesis like the one science shows us? That all this creation, with its galaxies and its stars, its planets and its lifeforms, its deep oceans and its towering mountains, its falls of water and its cliffs of ice, that *all this reality* could come from a point smaller than the head of a pin, a singularity so shrunken it has no radius, and that from this point that was not a point and this moment that was not a time there could explode a numinous fireball that had the searing energy of ten trillion suns.[15]

The seed of this fireball glowed with a heat that never was before or since. The gateway into time was a molten moment, where everything was focused together in total symmetry and brilliant, bright with a brightness that never was before or since.

Then, like a bubble, this fireball began to expand. Think of a drop of water on your palm; as it expands (evaporates) so it cools your skin. Just so, as this bubble got bigger it got cooler. A few minutes after Genesis its temperature had dropped enough to allow the first atoms to be created. Those genesis atoms were chiefly hydrogen, as we have seen, with some admixture of helium. Hydrogen is the simplest atom in the universe; it is the groundstuff of matter, the raw material of all evolution. The Canadian zoologist N.J. Berrill captured its significance in terms of the musical metaphor which is the motif of this book when he said:

> If you listen intently you can hear the universe singing its song of hydrogen, the first and the sustained note in the melody of creation.[16]

There are trillions of hydrogen atoms in our bodies. Thus the texture of our bodies and brains—the substance of our very being—is still continuous with an event that took place 15 billion years ago. We are still part of that 'great silent fire at the beginning of time'.[17] Each of us.

Hydrogen is the start of the evolutionary journey. In a typical star like the sun, hydrogen is burned to helium, the next highest element. This is the pattern. As the fires inside stars get hotter, as the furnaces of creation glow more brightly, so ever more complex elements can be created: carbon, oxygen, iron and so on. Our bodies are made of star-ash. *We are children of the stars*.[18] That may sound romantic but it is factually accurate. When we look at the diamond-pointed lights flecking the arching darkness of the night sky, when we feel, as human beings have done down the ages, an aching sense of connection, we are *remembering where we came from*. What we are 'now' is speaking to what we were 'then', each phase of our growth recognising the other in some dim way, below words.

> These bones, this hand
> star-ash
> brain molten with genesis heat.
> This quiet thought, that raging fire . . .[19]

Just as child and adult are different phases in the unfolding growth of the same entity, so star and human are different phases in the ongoing development of the one reality. As I have said elsewhere, the correct answer to a question concerning our ages as individuals is not to say 'I am 15 years old' or '34 years old' or '68 years old' as the case may be; rather, it is to affirm '*I am 15 billion years old*'.[20] This is our true age, the age of the universe, one of whose expressions we are.

This is the message of science to each of us and it is, I submit, stranger than anything the shamans of past ages taught their children: we are a star strangely and wonderfully fashioned into a thinking creature. *We are starstuff made conscious of itself.* We are a cosmos awakening in self-awareness, seeking to know what it *was* in order to understand what it *is*, so that it can look forward to what it *may be*.

Each culture has had its genesis myth, its song of creation. This is ours. It differs from its predecessors in a special way. It is, in a deep sense, *true*. We belong to the first generation of living things on this planet—as far as we know, in the universe itself—to understand its origins, to know the authentic answer to the ancient, aching question each child at some stage puts to its parent: '*Where did I come from?*'.

But even as it inspires so it also fails, for now an old issue comes back to haunt us. Being human, our minds demand of us an answer to the inevitable question; '*What came before the fireball?*'. Here we must abandon commonsense, for science says implacably that *time itself* 'began' in the quantum phantom in which reality had its genesis. As Paul Davies has put it, 'Time is not part of the stage on which the drama of creation is played out, it is one of the actors in the cast'.[21]

Our minds tend to rebel at this. Thinking as we do in our tense-structured language we simply cannot comprehend how what seems to us a fundamental given like 'time' could itself come into existence out of the blue. So let me put the question simply, as a child would put it, 'Where did the fireball really come from?'. And let me answer, equally simply. From nothing. Yes, from *nothing*.

That sounds so easy in mere words. But think of how the old myths of creation tell their story. The Bible says it like this:

> In the beginning . . . the earth was without form, and void; and *darkness* was upon the face of the deep. And the Spirit of God moved upon the face of the *waters*.

And the creation myth of the Maoris of New Zealand like this:

Io dwelt within the breathing space of immensity; the universe
was in *darkness*, with *water* everywhere.[22]

Notice how these two creation stories, which evolved so far
apart, in cultures which had no contact with each other, use
the same symbolism—darkness, water. Why? Because these are
the two most familiar images of nothing, of no-thing-ness;
darkness is the void in which nothing can be seen and water,
the ever-moving restlessness in which nothing can be fixed. So
the myth makers intuitively used them to describe the moment
before Creation, the shapeless womb before the world was.

For here contemporary science endorses the ancient message
of the sacred sense. At the root of all creation lies the paradox
we have already encountered, that *nothingness is full*, what
is *empty is also fertile*. This sounds contradictory in the language
of logic but not in the language of paradox because it is the
nature of paradox to reconcile opposites, as we have seen. To
tease out the cryptic message of this paradox imagine you are
sitting at a table on which you have put a brick. If you press
either your left or right hand against this brick it will move
because you bring energy—power—against it. However, if you
press equally on each end of the brick, it will stay still despite
the strength of your muscles. This is because, at the place where
your two hands meet the brick, the leftward power and the
rightward power are the same so, in a profound sense, there
is no power-that-can-be-used.

Let me expand on this with another metaphor. Think how
your body feels after a good meal. Suppose you have eaten
well and you have drunk good water. Your body is in balance.
You are not hungry, you are not thirsty. There is no reason
to move so you sit still and drowse. But after the night has
passed, when you wake to the cool promise of a new day,
there is an emptiness in your stomach. The balance is no longer
there. If you were a hunter in the olden days of the Aboriginal
Dreaming you would fetch your spear and rise, you would limber

your muscles and you would stalk the red desert, cool in the light of the just-rising sun. You would search out the bright-eyed lizard where it hides in the spinifex. You would find food and eat.

Hunger is a *breakdown of balance*. And this breakdown of balance summons up all the actions that will lead to the restoration of balance. The whole ritual of the hunt is called into being—created—by the simple fact of the breaking of balance. The breaking creates *desire* and where there is desire there is *will-to-action* and where there is *will-to-action* there is *power*.

In satisfying the body's hunger you return the balance to what it was; in satisfying the soul's hunger you return the balance to what it shall be. I hope you will understand this later, when we have investigated the strangeness of time.

The point I'm trying to make is simple: *any act of creation always comes from the use of unbalanced power*.

We can see a resonance of this truth in the structure of the human body.[23] There is a wonderful 4th century BC Greek statue called 'The Praying Boy' which captures this point better than any words (see Figure 3). Look at this boy's body; it is clean and strong, beautiful with the vigour of youth. Its curves and ripples are a kind of music. See this form in terms of this music. There is a deep *symmetry* in this shape; almost everything in this body comes in pairs—ears, eyes, arms, testicles, legs. What is more, these pairs have a crucially meaningful relationship to each other; each half of this body is a mirror image of the other.

Adjust your seeing to the symmetry of this rhythm. This symmetry is a balance, a balance split perfectly down the mid-line of the youth's body—except for the point where his limbs meet his loins. At this centre there is only one focus, the organ of his manhood, which by its very singleness, *violates the symmetry*. At this centre *the balance is broken*. And a broken balance is the source of power. Creative power. Always. This

22

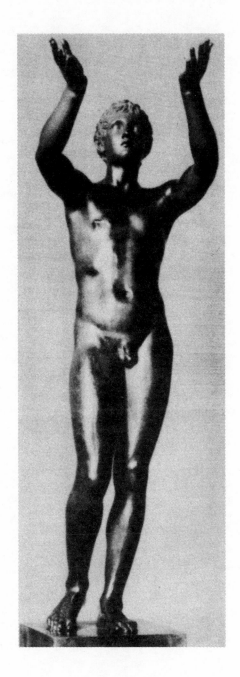

Figure 3 This 4th century BC statue of a praying boy exemplifies bilateral symmetry; that is, each half of his body is a mirror image of the other.

is why, in the Dreaming of all peoples, the phallus is a symbol of potency, a promise of becoming. This is why it is often hidden, beneath a loincloth on a body of flesh or a figleaf on a body of marble, lest this visible testament to the breaking of the balance disturb the balanced life of those who see it. The fact that, even today in Anglo-Saxon culture, it is forbidden by law to display an erect penis front-on in books, magazines or movies, is a powerful demonstration of the point I am trying to make.

Now concentrate on the other near-universal image of creation myths—water. Why did the prophets and seers of old sense that water told them something about beginnings? Think of the surface of a still stream. It is flat, it has no feature. In this featurelessness it is like darkness—a kind of nothingness, void of expression. Now watch a ripple take shape. To raise its crest it has to lower its trough. Its crest is made at the expense of its trough. In an exact way. The crest can only rear up as high as the trough sinks low. If you draw a line through the middle of a perfect wave you will see that the up-ness of the crest is equal to the down-ness of the trough (see Figure 4), so, if you take 'up' away from 'down' you get nothing, symbolised by the mandala sign O.

This example sets the paradoxical role of nothing in proper context. Nothing is the smooth surface of the level sea. Waves can form on this sea, this sea can become a whirlpool of activity because Nature can scoop from below what she wants to set on top. *But only for a flickering moment.* All this action has no strung-out-ness in time. The sea's creations have no permanence; they are seeds of time, no more. Nonetheless, however fleetingly they appear and disappear, they are *real*. Many real things do not last. Think of fire; think how flames leap and shimmer. You cannot 'hold' the shape of a flame for how can you hold something which has no extendedness in time? You never doubt, however, that flames are real, you never doubt their *power*.

24

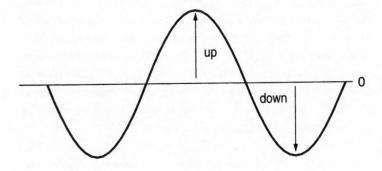

Figure 4 The paradoxical role of nothing (0). The crest of a wave can only rise as high as the base of its trough sinks low: 'up' and 'down' cancel out to give 0. Despite their creation from nothing, waves are real phenomena that help shape our world.

'Nothing' does not mean lack of power. Just the reverse. Because the energies that seethe in nothing are ephemeral, fleeting, ghostly, so precisely for this reason they are present everywhere and everywhen. So *nothing* contains the power to make *every*thing. The Void is full, the Void is fertile, Nothing is the womb of All.

The Void is what science calls a vacuum. It is the womb of Creation, the ghost realm whence come the players who will strut the stage of being, the emptiness which breeds infinity. The Void enfolds the very essence of paradox: a stillness that is ever in motion and a motion that is ever still; a ghost dance, whose spectral players dance forever on the forbidden edge of being; a dream that struggles to awaken into consciousness yet is ceaselessly drawn back into sleep; a phantom foam whose bubbles glimmer at the margins of 'where' and on the edges of 'when'; a premonition that aches to become a memory and a memory that aches to become a premonition; a dream that is all dreams; and none.

The vacuum is a sacred silence filled with profane noise. The noise that echoes in its emptiness is the voice of *randomness*, the signature of chance made manifest. This is the inner meaning of chance. Its utter fickleness gives it absolute freedom, making it the very root of creativity, the inexhaustible source from which all structure is drawn and into which all structure returns. So the message of emptiness is simple; *where nothing is present as form, everything is present as possibility*; all order is the gift of chance, all song is the gift of silence.

This treatment of the vacuum whispers to us softly, very softly, that the universe began as *a thought that dreamed itself awake*. So, using this fecund sense of what 'nothing' means, I am going to try to tell the story of creation in terms of a fable, a mythic metaphor. Think of two mountains, with smooth faces, bigger than anything you have ever dreamed. Each presses against the flat face of the other with such power, such power. Yet because they press in equal and opposite directions, in the place where they meet there is no unbalanced power.

Scale this power up to the limit of your imagination, until these flat surfaces have the focused force of a billion suns. Do not stop, keep going, keep going, increase the size of this power on and on, on and on, so that what presses against each other, in the point of exact balance, are forces that approach, although they do not reach, the powers of matched infinities. Where the almost limitless power of near-infinite strengths meet in exact balance the net force is O.

The trouble with this image is that we think of mountains as solid. So in your mind hold on to the thought of perfectly balanced power but let go of any idea of solidness. The balanced power exists in a *void*, it is invisible. And here is the revelation. At that pivotal place where the powers meet in balance there is a constant seething of minute motion. On the micro-scale, *the point of balance is never still*; glimmers of the briefest light, points of the finest matter, appear and disappear in an endless dance. This is the phantom world of the vacuum, this is the ghost dance, the haunted limbo where dreams boil on the forbidden edge of being, here is the sound of silence in all its profane noise.

Now I want you to cleanse your mind of another image. Clinging to the idea of balanced power in the void you are probably still thinking of the equal forces as made of matter, invisible matter. But this is too crude, for not only matter but *time* and *space* themselves are held in this matching balance. The flickerings of creation that seethe at the balance point are seeds of context as well as seeds of content. The ghost dance boils up to the brink of 'when' then retreats, just as it seethes to the edge of 'where' then dissolves.

We can see now where those ghost-specks of almost-being come from. A ghost can form *whenever the powers become unbalanced.* If a 'bulge' appears in the void on one side of the balance point, matter is sucked into being from the 'hole' it makes on the other side. Like a wave that buys 'up' by selling 'down', ghosts buy fleeting reality by trading *time* on one side of the balance for *essence* on the other.

Think of these balanced powers, these near-infinities that press together so that where they meet the power is O. Then imagine that a ghost-particle, a fleeting seed of space and time, does not flicker out of being but continues to grow. Such a violation of the hidden symmetry means that the *balance is broken completely.*

That violation is the *instant of Creation.* Here is how the thought awoke. Thus was the world born.

What does this mean? The answer is easy to set down in the symbolic language of mathematics and hard to articulate in words but, as always, the underlying truth is simple—the world came from nothing because it *is* nothing. The symbol—O—describes the situation where two mountains of almost unlimited size press equally against each other. There is power in O. Since O is just that, no-thing, the power in it is (almost) no-limit, (almost) infinite. In a strange way the universe is balanced like these matched near-infinities. The two forms of energy in the universe are equal and opposite so that, together, their net power is O.[24]

Everything in the universe we know is made of matter and matter is made of *atoms*. The same set of atoms, used in different combinations and structured in different patterns, makes all the richness of reality. Atoms are a very focused form of energy. We say this is *positive energy* because if the storehouse of energy in an atom is unlocked the essence it embodies is released in a mighty flash of power that has the very brightness of the sun itself. This is what happens in a hydrogen bomb.

But there is a secret built into this understanding and it is one of the deepest secrets science can teach us. At the beginning, at the instant of Creation, the universe possessed an absolute simplicity it has never had since. Time did not exist so there was no separation between past, present and future. There was no division of reality into matter and radiation. Even the forces that shape the world had not separated each from the other. The cosmos was a singular and perfectly symmetric unity.[25] *All was One.*

Then the universe began to unfold, its symmetries began to break, it 'exploded' in a sense, to start the story of evolution as we know it.[26] After the fireball had cooled enough, when the cosmos was three minutes old, atomic nuclei began to form, as I have already mentioned. But now we can again invoke metaphor and say that all atoms carry a 'memory' of the time they were together in undivided brightness. They desire to come together, to restore the union that was violated by the act of their birth. *All matter yearns to be one again.*

What is this yearning, this deep archetypal desire? You know it, I have but to speak its name and you will recognise it. We call this yearning *gravity*. This is why the principle of balance is so important because it points to the need for separation to be related to desire in an exact way. If two identical bits of matter are separated by the length of your body, their desire to come together can be represented by (for example) two straight sticks of equal size. If they are separated by twice the length of your body, their desire to reunite becomes a line which has the length not of two such sticks but of half a stick; that is, increasing the separation weakens the desire. By the same token, increasing the separation scales up the loneliness the fragments feel across the growing chasm of their separation. This loneliness, this need to come together is the precise measure of the gravitational energy coded into the gap that meters out the distance between the fragments.

This primal need for union—gravity—is universal. Even grains of light feel its insistent whisper. It is the all-permeating yearning of fragmented energy to again be one.

Gravity was the first child of time. It is the prime power that has made the world. Because of gravity fires burn inside stars, boomerangs soar high into the clear air and return precisely to the hand of their thrower, muscles lean on bone and tendon to create the flowing rhythm of running.

Just as the strength of this gravitational loneliness grows as divided matter is forced apart, so it diminishes as divided matter is brought together. To force bits of matter apart, one has to work against the power of their need to be together. As they come together, the loneliness they felt when separate diminishes. I can condense this into a simple rule: the amount of positive energy locked up in the total mass of the universe's divided matter is exactly the same as the amount of negative energy coded into the distances between the matter that is thus divided. So the net energy of the universe is O. To make the universe, one did not have to have something for nothing. Out of nothing came nothing. Yet that nothing was everything.

Hence, as always, a paradox. In the Creation the balance was broken. And preserved.

the image of
eternity

The question of origins raises, inevitably, the issue of *time*.
The genesis of time is as much a mystery as the genesis of
the universe itself. But the fact of time is such a basic part
of the structure of our everyday reality that we overlook the
fundamental strangeness of the thing it represents.

What is this phenomenon called time? Our experience of
it is of something that flows, that moves ever onward, that
carries us forward like a wave, that is forever trapped between
yesterday and tomorrow. This passing of time is a cornerstone
of the human condition. It is part of our sorrow; because time
passes quickly, so quickly, we grow old and die. The old Persian
poet, Omar Khayyam, spoke for all of us when he said of
the briefness of life:

> One moment in annihilation's waste,
> one moment of the well of life to taste—
> the stars are setting and the caravan
> starts for the dawn of nothing—oh, make haste![27]

But science speaks of a different reality. According to the
relativity theory of Albert Einstein, time cannot be teased apart

from space. The marriage of the two is a deeper phenomenon—spacetime.[28] And in the four-dimensional world of spacetime the distinction between past, present and future breaks down.

You can get inside the meaning of this by going outside and looking upward at the night sky, at a star. *When* do you see it? Now. But what does this mean? The light ripples that awaken the image of the star in your eye now may have left the star 40 million years ago. So what you see now, from the standpoint of your earth-centred limitation, is not the star that is but the star that was. You are looking at the past; when you look outward in space you look backward in time.[29]

Repeat this exercise, using not the eyes of your biological heritage but the eyes science has created, our instruments. Many of the artefactual eyes we use in science see realities our biological eyes are blind to. If we point sensitive radio-antennae in any direction in space we pick up a faint hiss. The technical name for this hiss that literally fills the cosmos is the 'microwave background radiation'.[30] This is the most ancient light there is, the sibilant after-echo of the fireball I spoke of before, the Genesis event in which the entire cosmos was born 15 billion years ago. So it is literally true that if we go outside and look at the sky with the eyes of our science, not the eyes of our skull, we can still see the fire that began the universe.

To go more deeply into this, I invite you to do something you may have read about in a science fiction book or seen in a movie. Put yourself in the mental position of a disembodied time-traveller 'riding' one of these ancient waves of almost exhausted light.[31] And ask the child-like question Einstein first asked, 'How does time look from the crest of a light wave?'. The answer is strange, so strange, yet it has that hidden logic that speaks of truth. The answer is that, at the speed of light, *time stops*.[32] So a non-material consciousness riding a lightwave created in the Big Bang would see the whole of the past simultaneously with the whole of the future.[33] To such a mind, the world's beginning would occupy the same moment as its end; there would be no before and no after—only an undivided now.

Superficially, this may sound outrageous. But try to remember something that even now may be tugging at your subconscious—the insights of the great visionaries of the human race, its mystics. When the German poet Johann Wolfgang von Goethe once wrote his famous line—*One moment holds eternity*—what was he giving voice to, if not this same insight that Einstein 'knew'?

If this representation of the illusionary nature of our human sense of time is hard to grasp, consider this analogy. You are in a car, on a drive. You pass a tree which then slips from sight around a corner. Does the tree cease to exist simply because you no longer see it? Of course not. If this analogy does not work for you let me try another. Imagine yourself in an elevator moving at uniform speed up a 40-storey skyscraper. Through the narrow window of the elevator you can see the various levels passing by in linear sequence—level 22, 23, 24—just as you feel time passing in linear sequence—two o'clock, three o'clock. But you know that level 22 doesn't cease to exist after you have passed it, just as level 45 is already in existence before you reach it. Just as the past is real, so is the future. This is not necessarily to say that the future is fixed and unchangeable in human terms. It is more like a landscape you can explore; which part of the landscape you see depends on the directions you take as a result of the choices you make.

If the past were somehow ground out of existence the moment you ceased to be aware of it, the universe would fall to pieces. Likewise, if the future were not already there for your experience to move into, the cosmos would not be coherent, that is, it would not 'hang together'. It is even obvious why you can't go back in time whereas you can move around in space. The universe is elegantly balanced between fixity and change, freedom and rigidity, choice and chance. Focusing on the fact that the universe is structured in four dimensions, it is clear that if you had complete freedom of action in all four there would be anarchy. As the ancient Greeks would have put it, 'instead of *cosmos* one would have had *chaos*'. So one dimension is not free—it has imprinted on it a one-way arrow that forbids you to go backwards, lest you undo the connections that hold the universe together. It so happens that this is the dimension we call time.

Somehow this fails to carry the conviction that comes from experience; it doesn't touch us in that inner space where our reality lives, where our mind's 'I' is. So I will try and relate this to you in a personal way. Think back to something you remember clearly, something you did recently that you enjoyed; suppose it was a morning you went swimming at your favourite beach.

Now, in your mind go back to that morning. Re-live it, feel again the salty tang of the breeze on your face, the glow of the sun on your cheek, hear the slapping of the wavelets on the sand. Now here is my message—the moment you are now reliving in memory *still exists*. In a literal, physical sense. In the four-dimensional spacetime landscape, that moment is still 'there', that past 'you' that so enjoyed that morning swim is still 'real'. *The past does not cease to exist simply because your mind moves beyond it*. No one moment is any more or less *real* than any other.

I need to make one extra point very clear. The person you 'were' that sunny morning is continuous with the person you 'are' now. Not only are all the moments that intervene between that past morning and now equally real, they are equally *democratic*—that is, no one moment is any more important than any other. The fleeting phantom we call 'now' matters to us only because our consciousness happens transiently to inhabit it. Moreover, this span of time is not divided up into intervals; the tracking systems (minutes, hours, days) we use to measure time are human inventions, not features of the real world. In actuality the person you are in the four-dimensional world of spacetime is a seamlessly unbroken process—what science calls a continuum.

The startling message is this; *only the continuum is real*. The you of the passing moment is a phantom, a reflection of the relatively lowly position we occupy in the spectrum of consciousness. We will delve more deeply into this concept in a later chapter.

This view of time changes the way we look at the world. Radically. And, in the same way, it simultaneously changes the way we look at ourselves. Indeed, we can now peel the first wrapping from the imaginary box that hides the metaphorical truth and we can approach our next question, which is our real question: *Who am I?*

And, as always when we look at things in an unsuperficial way, we touch a mystery. To move into this I invite you to go on a kind of guided meditation into your own physical person. Focus on the red corpuscles of your blood, the cells that let you breathe. Their red colour comes from a chemically symmetric molecule called haemoglobin; at the core of each haemoglobin molecule is an atom of iron. This iron was created in the fiery heart of a giant star.[34] So here is the question I want to put to you. What is the physical relationship between you and that star?

In your ordinary waking consciousness you think that the atom of iron in your blood now is something separate from its origin in the star. You think of the star as being remote in space and removed in time; it is 'there' while you are 'here'. But—and this is why I dwelt so long on the strangeness of time—the atom that was born in the star untold ages ago is *physically the same* atom that now helps you breathe. Far from being a 'grain' or 'speck' carried in the red cells of your blood, each atom of iron traces out a seamless line from its point of origin in a star to its point of position in your blood. *That unbroken continuum is the reality*. Each moment along that line—from creation to now—is democratically co-equal with all the others. They are a seamless 'worldline', one truth, just as the person you 'are' now is continuous with and part of the person you 'were' the morning you went swimming; one being, one truth.

Try and see yourself not in the false fiction of the passing moment but as an expanded consciousness would see you, in the timeless truth of the universe. The reality of an atom of iron is not the 'grain' you were taught of in school (that is a common illusion impressed upon you by the limitation of your vision); it is the unbroken oneness that stretches back to its origin. The atoms of iron that let you breathe are not merely the gift of a star, they are still *part* of a star. And what is true of the iron in your blood is true of the carbon in your liver, the phosphorus in your genes, the sulfur in your cartilage, the calcium in your bones. Thus, in a radically insightful way, science has made good the ancient intuition of the prophets: *I am the universe; the universe is my body.*

The Aboriginal Dreaming expresses this insight by saying that we are the earth and the earth is us. This sacred intuition can also be set in a scientific context. Each of the iron atoms that now resides in your blood most probably came from a plant. And the plant got the iron from the soil. So the unbroken line that is the reality of the atom of iron winds its way out across a journey more fantastic than the strangest dream of the wisest seer: it was smelted into being in the fiery furnace that was the brilliant core of a giant star; it was flung across space by the violence of a supernova when that star exploded in an apocalypse that had the brightness of a million suns; it congealed in the rocks of a just-born planet; it was rubbled into soil by wind and water and the action of microbes; it was taken up and made flesh by a plant; and now it lives in a red cell, circling the rivers of your blood, helping you breathe and keeping your consciousness afire, here, now.

From the fire of an exploding star to the fire of consciousness, one process, one being. In spacetime, each of us is not the body we identify as 'me'; rather we are each a dynamic world within a world. We do not merely sample the universe we live in, rather we are seamlessly part of that universe. We are the gift of many stars, the flesh of many creatures, the waters of many rivers; we are the rocks of the mountain, the red earth of the desert, the iris of the eagle's eye, the apple of the orchard, the venom of the snake. *We still are all we once were. And perhaps we already are all we ever shall be.* Time is the illusion and unity, the profound insight that 'All is One', is the truth of the universe.

When we look back in time we remember who we are, knowing that our past selves do not lie like discarded images in some vanished space or scratched-out moments in some forgotten time. The reality of who we are is made up of and illuminated by all the former selves on whose shoulders we now stand. As the poet Kathleen Raine says:

> As you leave Eden behind you, remember your home,
> for as you remember back into your own being
> you will not be alone; the first to greet you
> will be those children playing by the burn,
> the otters will swim up to you in the bay,
> the wild deer on the moor will run beside you.
> Recollect more deeply, and the birds will come,
> fish rise to meet you in their silver shoals,
> and darker, stranger, more mysterious lives
> will throng about you at the source
> where the tree's deepest roots drink from the abyss.
>
> Nothing in that abyss is alien to you.
> Sleep at the tree's root, where night is spun
> into the stuff of worlds . . .[35]

This is our journey then, to try and escape the trap of time that imprisons our consciousness in this fictional monolayer of experience we call the passing moment. So that we can see the world whole, as it truly is, One World, without end.

Chapter 3

the ticking of the clock

In the last chapter I spoke of the universe as 'timeless'. But this is not the way we know the world. We have a subjective sense of the *flow* of time. Each day is different. The numbers on the digital readout of our watches seem to track the passage of a movement that is basic to our entire experience. What is the explanation for this sense of the movement of time?

I believe the origin of the sense of time passing is tied up with the origin of language. Language is a thing of power; it is what brings minds into contact, it allows new insights to outlive the mind that discovers them. Yet language is also a barrier to, not a vehicle of, knowing. The Chinese sage Lao Tzu summed up this paradox when he said: *he who knows does not speak; he who speaks does not know.* What does this mean? It flows from the one deep insight, which I will come back to over and over again during our time together, the insight that All is One.

Let us think this through. If all is truly one, nothing can be separate in truth. If we see it as separate, we are divided from it by something that is a lie and that something is usually bound up with our sense of a separate self.

This, in essence, is what language is—an attempt to build bridges between our separate selves. But words are corrupted by the same fault as the minds that make them; they are fragments, vehicles of possible knowing, not knowing itself. Words usually only make sense together, as all meaning must, but their togetherness does not show itself as 'oneness' in the sense of the deep insight that All is One; rather their togetherness is the togetherness of markers whose connection is the serial way they are stretched out along the trail of time. We can only pass the markers one at a time; we cannot know them in their all-at-onceness, at the same moment.

Consider this spoken sentence: 'What I am saying consists of eight words'. You (the listener) cannot know that the sentence I am speaking will contain only eight words until I have finished saying it. You cannot understand the intended meaning of the first word in the sentence until the last has been reached. Each word only makes sense in relation to what comes *before* and *after*. Thus you have to hold a memory of each successive word in your mind to make sense of the whole. Each individual sound-symbol must be heard in the context of a *past* and a *future* to convey meaning. Moreover, the set of sound-symbols must be said by the speaker and heard by the listener *in sequence*. For the whole to be understood there is an inescapable requirement for a movement of concentration along a string of units (sounds) linked by the order in which they are spoken.

It is my belief that the sequential inner sense of the movement of time mimics this sequential inner sense of the movement of speech because these two aspects of our subjective life are indissolubly interwoven.

To understand the meaning of any sentence it is essential that any given word in the set is successively removed from the focus of our attention so that the next word can be grasped and processed in a way that preserves the flow of experience. This serial ordering—bringing into focus (from the future state), holding (present state) and eliminating (past state)—is the very basis of the continuity of speech. What I am suggesting is that it is also the basis of the continuity of time because the sequential this-after-that structuring which makes speech possible is a major source of the this-after-that structuring that creates our human sense of the passage of time. It is largely language that gives birth to both anticipation and recall.

This explanation for the origin of our sense of time suffers from what seems to be a fatal flaw—it is, in the eyes of many, too simple. We are so programmed to structure our thoughts in the linear sequences that language requires that we find it almost impossible to step outside the process and compare verbal and nonverbal modes of consciousness. However, this verbal (and other conceptual) programming is sometimes interrupted during lapses of concentration and it is noticeable that these moments of self-forgetting absorption typically affect our sense of time's passing, as witnessed in statements like 'Oh, I lost track of time for a moment'. Deep meditation also eliminates the busy flux of conceptual processing and it is characteristic of the still state of meditational consciousness that all sense of time passing is lost. One of the hallmarks of a 'good' meditation is that there is, in that quietened awareness, no sense of inner time even though the clock that reads 2.00 p.m. when we enter a meditational trance may read 3.30 p.m. when we 'come to'.

Despite this, we are still left with the feeling that this explanation is much too facile to explain the origin of something as basic as our sense of time. Let me emphasise, therefore, that there is no equivalent phenomenon anywhere in biology or physics; sequential, A—B—C—D 'time-lapse' processing is unique to the mechanism of conceptualisation. In evolutionary terms it can emerge only when the 'now'-focused, survival-oriented responses of animals give way to the temporally delayed responses of humans, which uncouple behaviour from survival strictures and allow a completely new existential dimension—thought—to emerge. The significance of this is summed up in the statement 'Man is the only animal who can be highly active while sitting still'.[36]

Just as importantly we must never lose sight of the critical evolutionary 'break-through' that language represents. In the accessible universe there are only two known mechanisms for remembering—for storing and transmitting information.[37] The first is words, the second genes. Thus data stored in spoken or written words can be replicated across successive generations of human brains just as data stored in genes can be replicated across successive generations of living cells. Language is just as much a mode of heredity as DNA and RNA.[38] The origin of language is thus on an exact par, from the point of view of its evolutionary significance, with the origin of genes. So perhaps it is not too surprising that the beginnings of language should correlate so strongly with the beginnings of that other taproot feature of our human way of structuring the world of our experience—time.

All this suggests that our sense of time must depend critically upon the brain processes that underpin mechanisms of short-term memory. A tragic story hints that this is indeed so. In 1985, a world expert on Renaissance music, Clive Wearing, contracted the herpes virus that causes cold sores. Herpes viruses infect nerve cells and in this unusual case the virus selectively attacked and destroyed a structure (the hippocampus) deep inside Clive's brain. As a result, Clive lost his sense of past time completely; he now lives in an eternal present moment, convinced that he has only just awakened from a long period of unconsciousness. The diary which he obsessively keeps reveals his frantic search to regain some sense of the continuity of time that we take for granted, giving us an insight into the nightmare world that results when it is lost:

9.04 Now I am AWAKE

10.00 NOW I AM AWAKE

10.28 ACTUALLY I AM NOW FIRST TIME AWAKE[39]

. . . and so on, ad infinitum.

Clive can still speak so the brain damage responsible for his condition cannot be the primary site of the time-structuring mechanism I have been talking about. A better window of insight may come from patients who have suffered damage to the 'speech centres' of the brain as a result of strokes and other conditions or injuries. Injury to a specific area of the brain's outer layer (the cerebral cortex), called *Wernicke's centre*, cripples the ability to understand language. In the particular case of what is technically known as conduction aphasia patients cannot repeat words.[40] This suggests that the brain damage they have sustained touches on the mechanisms that program our this-after-that speech ordering and, hence, our this-after-that time-ordering capabilities. This is almost certainly only a small part of the answer however (if indeed it is linked at all) because language calls into play diverse regions of the brain. It seems significant to me that patients with damage to their frontal lobes have difficulty sequencing their actions over time. Goal-oriented behaviour is especially affected, as if patients have become incapable of remembering their intentions.[41] The perception of time is intimately affected in these situations but evidently not in any simple way.

So, at the time of writing, the neurological basis of our sense of time is still a puzzle. But the point of this chapter remains: the passage of time is a function of the present evolutionary construction of our brains, an invention of our psyches, *not a feature of the physical universe*. If you stand by a waterfall you can watch water flow. With the right tools you can measure the rate of its flow. But you cannot measure the rate of flow of time with any instrument, because time does not exist except in the sequenced flux of your thoughts, as part of the way you have learnt to deal with the symbolic world your mind makes through language.

This is difficult and unfamiliar territory, the more so because it places the very mechanism I am using to communicate with you—language—in the role of 'maya', the weaver of illusion.

41

So let us return to Lao Tzu's words: *He who knows does not speak; he who speaks does not know.* What this means, at least in part, is that speech is fatally flawed because it seeks to recreate in sequential pieces the all-at-once fullness of an insight that usually is destroyed by the very act of speaking it. As I have just explained, the listener is caught in a two-edged cleft in respect of each word; he or she must remember what went before and anticipate what comes after. Each word has to be both a premonition and a memory of its neighbours. Speech tries to build in time what can only be known when there is no time. This is why the act of speech marks us out as human; it makes us higher than the beasts but keeps us lower than the gods.

To make messages in words, your mind must take its integrated thoughts apart, transform the 'sub-units' into fractured sound-symbols which represent the divided-up memory of the undivided knowing, then speak the pieces into the ear of the hearer in the hope that, from these sounds, he can put together again in his mind the knowing that was in your mind. But he cannot; the togetherness he makes in his mind will not be the togetherness that was in your mind. How could it be?

Let me use a parable that I have found useful. Words are like stones dropped into a pond. *What conveys meaning is not the stone but the ripple it sends out.* A point of this parable is that the surface of the pond must be still and flawless if the meaning one seeks to convey is not to be corrupted in the act of conveyance. If winds blow across the surface of the water, ripples set up by stones will be weakened by cross-currents and meaning will tend to be lost. Interference between conflicting wave forms makes communication difficult if not impossible.

Before you say anything there must be in your mind a focusing—you must work out what it is you want to say. In terms of the metaphor, in the waters of your mind thought waves ripple towards an idea. Those waves can only transmit their message faithfully if the medium through which they propagate is undisturbed; the meaning they encode is distorted if they are forced to ripple through water in a different state or at a different level. So here is what I think happens when you speak. To carry your thoughts across the divide that separates speaker from listener, you must 'collapse' the spread-out ripples of your thoughts into the sharp-edged sounds you call words, sending sounds as signals across the gap you wish to bridge. When these words are dropped into the water of the listener's mind they set up ripples in that mind and these ripples also converge into an idea. But because the mind of the receiver is almost certain to be in a different state, the resulting ripples make a different pattern, which means they make a different idea.

Speech is an endless balancing act, forever falling off the edge of understanding. When you hear a person speak, you must listen for each separate word in turn so you can link what comes before with what comes after. You have no choice because meaning comes only from the pattern of togetherness. As all meaning does. Only togetherness tells truly; all separation speaks a lie. The poet Robert Graves got it right when he said:

> Naming is treacherous
> for names divide
> truths into less truths,
> enclosing them in a coffin of counters
> give the spell no name![42]

Speech is a clumsy thing, a badly made tool. Speech is a frail reed reaching out across the gap between minds; it makes contact possible but the message it carries is crippled by the very act of crossing. The only knowing that has depth is that which occurs without between-nesses, when there is no gap between speaker of and spoken to. This is the completed act of love when two souls who, in words, thought they were separate, in knowing, see they are one.

Chapter 4

a tale of two flowers

The preceding two chapters have dealt with time in its contradictory aspects of being and becoming. As 'being' (duration), time seems static, something that is simply 'there', but we know it as 'becoming', clock time. To resolve these and other matters, we need to peel another wrapping from the box that holds the truth, and look again at our root question: 'Who am I?'. We can only do this by examining a revolution that has occurred in the past 30 years or so, leading science to affirm the very attitudes it once denied. This revolution focuses on *mind* and on the vexed question: 'What is real?'.

The old science of Newton fundamentally misled us about the nature of reality. We used to think that things were only real if they were solid. We spoke of 'solid matter' and we defined the practical world in the reassuring bricks-and-mortar terms that conformed so comfortably to our everyday experience. We now know this is utterly wrong. We have understood for over 50 years that the atoms which make up solid matter are over 99.99 per cent *empty space*. Somehow we have absorbed this without letting it alter the way we see. But the branch of science we call quantum mechanics has pricked the bubble of our whole concept of reality, letting in alien thoughts, strange beyond dreaming, known to be true when encoded in mathematical symbols but forever barred from the mental landscape of everyday life.

In the old story science used to tell, an atom was commonly thought of as a tiny particle like a miniature billiard ball. So, like a billiard ball, an atom should obey Newton's laws of mechanics along with all the other 'solid' things that occupy our commonsense world. The same should apply to still smaller subatomic particles like electrons.

Let us follow this through. According to Newton, a particle like an electron should have a precise mass and a precise velocity, and these two measurable quantities should allow us to predict its future behaviour in a deterministic way. But when science peered deep down into the basic structure of matter this predictable behaviour melted away like an illusion. It is a basic rule of quantum mechanics that you cannot determine the position and momentum of an electron at the same time; if you define one, the other becomes fuzzy and ghostly and vice versa.[43]

This is not a failure of our instruments, not a flaw of technique—it is an inbuilt feature of Nature's design. An electron does not have a defined position and momentum.[44] An unobserved electron exists not as a particle as we thought, not as a minuscule ball of matter, but as a *wave*. And not a physical wave like the waves that roll on to the beach. Something more subtle, a wave of potential, *a ripple of possibility* . . .

At the taproot level, 'solid' matter evaporates into a ghost, a glimmer of something just glimpsed over the hill, a flirtatious 'maybe' hovering at the edge of being, something more like an expectation than a substance, a dream that needs the stiffening touch of human will to summon it into the realm of reality, to tease it into time.

This is unfamiliar territory to most people so let me try and make it simple. Imagine you are looking out the window at an iris in the garden, admiring its deep blue colour. I come into the room beside you and give you a photo which shows the iris as seen through the eye of a bee. Straight away you are puzzled. Not only is the flower no longer blue, it is streaked with strange markings on the petals, a grid of inward-pointing lines that makes you think, irresistibly, of a runway. It is a different flower, you protest. But it is not, it is the same flower seen through a different eye. The bee's eye, unlike yours, can see ultraviolet light. So the bee's eye sees what its genes have trained it to see—a grid of markings, a landing track, to guide it to the source of the flower's nectar. This pattern is invisible to you because your eye is not made to access this higher-energy end of Nature's rainbow of colours.

So which image of the flower is correct—yours or the bee's? Here is the point of the parable, they both are! No one image is 'correct'; each is tailored to the needs of the creature which sees it. What of a different eye again? Yes, it would see yet another kind of flower. And here is the mind-expanding truth of it: *the process has no limit.* The 'reality' of the flower is an endless bundle of possibilities, a many-faceted treasure. What appears at the invisible interface between seer and sight is only a single option drawn from a lottery that is mathematically inexhaustible.

Each different eye sees a different flower and each different flower is a face of the 'real' flower. None is any more or any less authentic than the others. We unconsciously think that our human image of the flower is special, is 'better', but this is merely a reflection of our own arrogance. The bee would think the same—or the weasel or the eagle—to each of whom the flower would reveal a different face of its limitless essence.

Seeing depends on sight. But there are other senses, so I will give you another metaphor that may resonate more 'truly' for you. Imagine you are listening to the strains of Pachelbel's popular Canon and Fugue in D, letting the magic of the music sing to you as you read. Now you have brought the 'shape' of the song in your mind I want you to ponder this. If you heard this melody played only on a cello would you recognise it? Of course! On a violin? Of course. On a flute? Of course. Each different instrument creates a different singing of the same song. Each instrument tells a different version of the same theme. In this case, it is not the ear which hears but the instrument that plays that defines the kind of song we hear.

In terms of this metaphor, a quantum ripple is like a full orchestra and choir with a literally limitless repertoire of instruments, each playing a different version of a common theme. All the notes blend faultlessly together to make the chorus of creation, but *there is no ear on earth that can hear the complete symphony*. Not yet. At this present stage of evolution all the creatures of this earth hear but a few notes from the combined chorus; they recognise the tune without hearing the music.

To start to see where all this takes us it is necessary to look away from the message of quantum mechanics to the science that made it possible. In the West our image of reality has been deeply, irreversibly, influenced not only by the fruits of the scientific quest but by the attitudes it generated. What I mean shows through clearly from an examination of the scientific method. Science operates by a strategy of analysis, which requires it to *separate* the object to be studied from all 'extraneous' elements, to segregate it from the rest of the universe, in a test-tube or cabinet. The unspoken assumption behind this is that observer and observed are separate phenomena.

It is important to stress how axiomatic this assumption is and how deeply it colours our thinking. The idea that a human mind can experiment with Nature in such a way that the experimenter does not influence the outcome of the experiment lies at the core of the scientific method; it is the basis for the doctrine of 'objectivity'. This doctrine has paramount status in our culture, not just in physics but in the so-called social sciences that look to 'hard science' for their validation. This assumption is pervasive, powerful, accepted—and wrong.

Here is where the core message of quantum physics comes into compelling focus. Stripped of its complexities, the point of this chapter is simply this, that the act of observation changes the nature of the thing observed, that *observer and observed, far from being separate, are coupled in the most intimate of ways*. Physicist John Wheeler summed up this radical refocusing in these words:

> Nothing is more important about the quantum principle than this, that it destroys the concept of the world as 'sitting out there', with the observer safely separated from it by a twenty-centimetre slab of plate glass. Even to observe so minuscule an object as an electron, he must shatter the glass. He must reach in . . . Moreover, the measurement changes the state of the electron. The universe will never afterwards be the same. To describe what has happened, one has to cross out that old word 'observer' and put in its place the new word 'participator'.[45]

Precisely because it comes from the direction they least expect it, namely science itself, the quantum message is very threatening to people who still live within the subject/object duality, so let me try and explain it in my own language. By its own terms of reference, science attempted to set itself apart from the mental processes that made its successes possible. But this separation was never achievable, even in principle. Facts, items of awareness, only gain meaning if they are brought together into statements or theories. Yet the very act of integration that produces a theory draws on an invisible software of shared assumptions and unconsciously accepted value judgements and this subliminal software creates the mindset we inhabit. This mindset, this neural programming, was written by natural selection and by our own past experience. It is thus not, in any sense, absolute; it can and must and does reflect where we come from.

This is the often-said but seldom understood message of

A TALE OF TWO FLOWERS

quantum physics—simple and shattering—that *the data has no meaning separate from the software that organises it.* There is no such thing as an uninterpreted 'fact'.

There has been great resistance to the quantum concept. Here, perhaps more than anywhere else, we reach a point in the history of human understanding where science does not want to look at the inner meaning of its own discoveries. For the essence of the quantum message is a simple revelation: *consciousness enters into the structure of reality in a fundamental way.*[46]

This conclusion follows logically and inevitably from our discussion of what an electron is. An electron encodes the kind of contradiction that spells out my whole approach in this book. In its very essence, an electron is a paradox since it seamlessly unites two (apparently) mutually exclusive opposites, being simultaneously wave and particle.

Only in the particle the wave;
only in the wave the particle.

The universality of this wave/particle duality at the subatomic level gives point to Bohr's belief (see Introduction), that 'opposites are not contradictory but complementary'. It has taken the Western mind centuries to grasp what the Eastern has understood for thousands of years—that reality is better described in terms of both/and rather than either/or.

The fascinating aspect of this 'reality paradox' is the hinge role that mind plays. In the absence of consciousness the electron exists as a wave; in the presence of consciousness it exists as a particle. Thus *it is the consciousness of the intelligent observer that determines which of these two alternative realities an electron will incarnate at any one time.*[47]

We will discuss this hinge aspect of quantum physics in the next chapter. At the moment I am less concerned with the facts of the quantum message than with their consequences. Why is the quantum perspective so threatening? Because it makes the structure of our experience, the very focus from which we view the world, begin to flicker at the margins, so that what we thought was solid and secure becomes the glimmer-image of a surreal fantasy, glimpsed as a memory in a stranger's dream.

We reach here a critical point in our quest for understanding. Up to now we have been able to treat knowledge as though it were objective and value-free, we have been able to ask for understanding as a child asks, not knowing the consequences of its own curiosity. With modern physics we start to rediscover an ancient truth, that there is a price to everything, and with quantum mechanics we start to intuit just how awesome this price may be. *The price is the entire structure of our concept of reality.* Once we grasp the full implications of the quantum message we can never again naively believe that the world we *see* is the world that *is*; instead we are confronted with a much more challenging assertion, that the world we see is the world we *make*.

Remember what I said at the beginning of this book? Each time a layer of wrapping is removed from our metaphorical box, each time a new insight possesses our minds, we change, we become different people. This is the nature of knowing, that a major advance in understanding, aptly dubbed a quantum leap, destroys the very awareness it replaces. *One cannot grow and stay the same.*

What does this mean in personal terms? At this particular moment in time you have a particular sense of 'I am' based on the way you integrate the experiences you have had. This is the mind's 'I' that inhabits the eyes that are currently reading these words. This 'I' seeks to preserve itself at all costs, because it is the self-sustaining focus of your inner life, the organising lens through which you view the world. This is where *fear* enters the picture, for a radical shift in consciousness resulting from a critical new insight can and will and must destroy this self. The 'I' you have been *dies*.

Older cultures saw the search for knowing in terms of what the great mythologist Joseph Campbell has described as a 'hero's journey'.[48] In all times and in all cultures there have been rare, gifted individuals who sought to know more than the wisdom of their time could tell them. Such seekers cut themselves off from their people, they went alone into high places or lonely valleys, they fasted, they underwent great hardships. The torments their bodies endured were a reflection of the torments their psyches experienced. In their imaginations they were burned by otherworldly fire, shown strange sights, haunted by dark demons and enraptured by music so powerful it can compel a world. It was understood by all people in olden times that this journey of the soul was a journey of great risks.

But those who came back from the hero's journey were men of knowing, shamans, who had the gift of sight and the power of healing. They became the wise ones of their tribe, having paid in full the terrible price their gods demanded, the sacrifice of self. T.S. Eliot understood perfectly the nature of this sacrifice when he spoke of 'a condition of complete simplicity, costing not less than everything'.[49]

What is the hero's journey of our age? Ninja games on a computer screen? Voyages to far-off suns on the star-ship 'Enterprise'? Ours is the age of make-believe, which sends substitute heros on risk-free journeys into virtual realities. Yet the hero's journey is still there, as it has always been and as it always will be, ever beckoning to those who have the courage to answer to its call. It is not the call to discovery in the old sense for on earth at least—except in matters of detail— the seas are all charted, the mountains are all climbed and the jungles are all conquered. The frontier now lies in the psyche, at the very point we have reached in our journey together. If we venture beyond this point we may voyage into the unmapped territory that lies beyond it, which is 'the mystery of what we have not yet become'.[50]

But the equations of the inner universe are as mathematically exact as those of the outer, so the *promise* of this journey into your self's potential is symmetrically matched by the *risks* it entails. As the poet Gerald Manley Hopkins so cogently understood, the landscape of the mind has its own terrors:

> Oh the mind, mind has mountains; cliffs of fall
> frightful, sheer, no-man-fathomed.[51]

So to willingly embark on a voyage of discovery into the unrealised promise of your own mystery is to accept that your footsteps will often teeter on the brink of unease and may sometimes falter on the edge of terror. We can slay the beasts of the jungle with the weapons of our technology but we cannot slay the beasts of our imagination with any weapons except the truth of our own integrity.

What the hero's journey requires of us today is no more and no less than it required of the seekers of long ago. As ever, it summons up our courage to face the dark dissolution of *death itself*. The call to self-realisation is the siren's voice of the Lorelei, tempting us to sacrifice all that we are on the altar of all that we can become.

Chapter 5

falling into time

In the first three chapters we looked at the world in the way we are accustomed to looking at it, treating it as though it were 'external' to ourselves. But the last chapter turned us around 180 degrees for, with our treatment of quantum mechanics, we had of necessity to start to look inwards, probing into the mental universe, where our thoughts sparkle in the capricious dance of consciousness.

We now face the key question of the relationship between the world without and the world within. Which brings us to the basic fallacy of the way we see. Because the eyes of our skulls look outwards at the world in front of us, we mistake that picture of the world for the world's reality. What we forget is that the picture we see before our eyes is woven *behind* our eyes, inside our brains. In terms of a computer analogy, it is the mental program that integrates the data we receive, not the receiving organ (eye) which permits us to see. We see with our software, which means that *our reality can only be as good as the software we bring to it.*

The simplest way to summarise the quantum revelation is to say that the world 'out there' and the world 'in here' are inextricably interwoven. Straight away this generates a crisis of identity. The question 'Who am I?' takes on a radically different meaning when we realise that we cannot—even in theory—separate the mind that sees from the thing that is seen. In this chapter I will try to meet the challenge of that crisis, by going into the depths of our minds to make plain the meaning my words have hinted at.

The question which arises is obvious: 'What *is* mind if it has this awesome power to create a world?'. In even attempting to answer this question in a sensible way I am at once tied down by the limitations of language. So, as before, I will use the imagery of metaphor and say, simply: *Mind is the bridge between formlessness and form.*

What does this mean? It means that the quantum wave, the ripple of possibility, does not, in an important sense, exist any*where* or any*when*; that is, it does not inhabit the space/time construct we experience in our familiar, everyday world. In the absence of mind, of eyes to see, all ripples of possibility exist as unresolved composites of superposed 'options' so, in the absence of mind, the wave-like sub-text of the world of your reality is formlessly present, like a song that waits for a singer to sing it.

Moreover, the world of the quantum ripple is symmetric in a way our everyday world is not. A ripple of possibility can vibrate from the past to the future, like our human sense of time; or, equally, it can vibrate from future to past. To put it more precisely, the mathematical equation that describes it, like most laws of physics, is time-reversible; it contains no inbuilt arrow of time.[52]

What happens when you 'look'? What is the alchemy that is wrought by that moment of seeing? The truthful answer is that we do not know. Somehow the act of observation changes the basic structure of the quantum wave. The wave/particle duality is resolved in favour of the particle. The ripple of possibility becomes the fixedness of fact, the spread-out wave form becomes the sharp-edged object, the unrealised option becomes the realised choice. In scientific language we say that the act of seeing 'collapses the wave function' of the quantum ripple,[53] giving form to what previously was formless, making real what previously was merely possible.

Each act of seeing creates a world. It does not matter whether the eye that sees is that of a weasel or an eagle or a sea horse; it is the intervention of mind—on any level—that summons forth a universe. And here is the key point: each act of seeing, in the very act of creating a world, *traps it in time*, extracting essence from the time-symmetric realm of quantum possibility and ensnaring it in matter, in our familiar one-way world of space and time, where things grow old and die.

Notice how this tends to reverse the old order of things! We used to think—we still do in everyday life—that mind was flimsy and ephemeral, a dream-image, and that matter was real and permanent. Now we hover on the brink of a revelation that makes measurable matter the stuff that dreams are made of—almost literally—while measureless mind becomes the rock on which perception is built. In my view (and mine is a perception only a minority of physicists will agree with[54]), mind is primary and the familiar 'givens' of the outer world are constructions we fashion from gossamer, sculpting realities from mathematical smoke rings, picking options from the ghostly lottery of quantum possibility by means of our own actions and trapping them in time.

What does this mean? To get into this topic we need to delve more deeply into the linked question with which we began the last chapter: 'What is real?'. We humans are so arrogantly confident about the 'reality' of what we see around us. We touch the smooth surface of a tabletop and say without question, 'This is *solid*, this is *real*'. But we forget the relativity of sight. To a flea the table top would not be smooth; it would be corrugated into a fantastic landscape of peaks and valleys. And think how a recent portrait photograph of you would vanish as you went from the human scale of seeing to the flea's, how the familiar contours of your face would explode into a wilderness of black and white boulders. The flea would see this landscape of boulders as stable but to a small microbe the chemical fretwork of each knoll and shallow would shimmer in the random dance of a motion that never stopped. As the physicist Lecomte du Nuoy said, '*It is the scale of observation that creates the phenomenon*'.[55]

A central part of our problem is that because 'reality' is a single word, we think of it as if it were a single or uniform state. In our scientific culture we act as though the everyday reality we experience when we are awake is the *only* reality. But this is nonsense, there are other 'realities'—for example, the realm we glimpse in dreams. When we dream we enter a different quality of reality; in dreams we can fly on wings we do not have, see impossible visions, confront monsters, move from image to image without the 'waiting' that is a feature of the linear time of ordinary experience.

'In reality', there is an infinity of different 'realities'. Each species of creature on this planet has its own reality, which means that it samples quantum ripples in its own special way, painting its own particular picture of the world in its own individual 'mind'.

Many people will reject this. They will insist that there is only one reality which various creatures tap into in different ways. This raises an issue that is central to everything which follows. Let me give you a metaphor that I will use throughout the rest of this text. This metaphor is very rich but it must never be taken literally. I have been describing reality in terms of waves, ripples, because waves are part of its deep nature. But the subtle vibrations of quantum ripples lie outside our everyday experience. So let me use the analogy of the waveset most familiar to us, the light we use to see, noting that the mathematics which describe light waves can be remarkably similar to the mathematics that describe quantum waves; indeed, if we restrict our attention to a single 'particle' of light, then the equation that describes the quantum wave becomes the equation that describes the light wave.[56]

Light can be described as a vibration, a set of waves with peaks and troughs (see Figure 5). The distance between peaks is called the wavelength of the light and the number of times the crest of a wave passes a given point per second is called the frequency of the light wave. When white light passes through a prism, it breaks up into a rainbow of colours technically called a spectrum; what goes in as 'one' comes out as 'many'. Each colour in the spectrum has its own characteristic wavelength: energy-poor light has a long wavelength—we see it as red; energy-rich light has a short wavelength—it constitutes the blue waveband. A bee can see beyond the visible spectrum into an even more energy-rich band called ultraviolet. The example is not important but the principle is: *different eyes see different frequencies.*

So let us sketch out a spectrum of light energies, in terms of their associated wavelengths.

long wavelength	low energy	red light
medium wavelength	medium energy	green light
short wavelength	high energy	blue light
all wavelengths	all energies	white light

Let us now bring eyes and minds into the picture. It is a feature of optics that eyes can only discriminate between separate objects in their field of vision if the wavelength of the light is less than the distance between the objects to be discriminated. This is dubbed the resolving power of an eye.

So far this is all good science. But now I want to use this spectrum of light as a metaphor for a concept that may at first seem strange—the concept of *a spectrum of reality.* I will justify my use of this metaphor as I move through the remaining pages of this book. At the moment all I need to stress is that

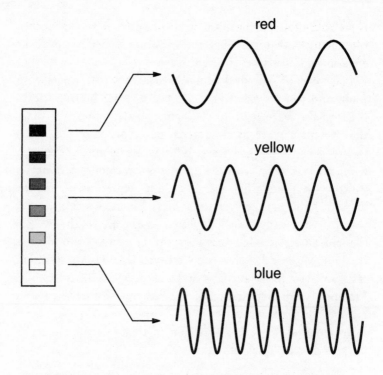

Figure 5 The electromagnetic spectrum; the various colours in the narrow band of the spectrum we see as light are differentiated on the basis of the frequency of their vibrations, that is, the number of wave crests that pass a given point per unit of time. The higher the frequency the more energy the light has.

each graduated 'level of reality' depends on the 'wavelength' of the 'light' that is accessible ('visible') to its associated level of consciousness through its relevant organ(s) of perception. The consciousness that 'sees' light only on the energy-poor ('red') wavelength sees a coarse-grained reality since it cannot resolve most of the data in its surroundings; it cannot see the richness of the world. The consciousness that 'sees' middle-energy light sees a more clearly defined reality as its 'eyes' can resolve more elements. The consciousness that 'sees' the energy-rich 'blue' has a highly accurate image of reality since it sees its environment in fine-grained detail.

What are these levels of reality? The major 'bands', the key 'wavelengths' in this rainbow of reality and the associated 'rainbow of consciousness' are:

low-frequency	physical reality	all sub-human states of consciousness
mid-frequency	mental/waking reality	ordinary human consciousness
high-frequency	imaginal/dreaming reality	symbolic and non-ordinary states of consciousness
all frequencies	unitary reality	no-boundary consciousness

It is important to remember that this is only a metaphor and not to get carried away with ideas associated with any literal interpretation. The principle is what matters and the principle is an allegorical extension of the axiom set out before: different *eyes* see different *wavebands* see different *worlds*.

In terms of the metaphor, waking consciousness is like, say, the yellow band of the spectrum. I believe that in our ignorance of what consciousness is, we have assumed until now that this narrow window is the only consciousness there is. So we have nourished a view of reality so impoverished it has crippled the very roots of our seeing. What I am suggesting now is that consciousness is much richer than this, that it contains and encompasses an entire spectrum whose layers extend both 'above' and 'below' the mindset we are used to. But Nature does not recognise the separateness of categories as we do. We talk of 'red' and 'blue' as separate colours, yet in reality they shade imperceptibly into the other colours that make up the continuum of the spectrum. Just so, each level in the continuous rainbow of reality is permeable to the others. In waking consciousness we are sometimes haunted by images or premonitions from the world of dreams, from the dreaming state. Our language reflects this; when we slip momentarily out of waking consciousness we say we 'daydream'.

If these other realities exist, *where are they*? It is such an inevitable question. Yet the possibility of a 'spectrum of reality' is so much in line with our experience. Each day in the USA hundreds of radio stations broadcast non-stop messages into the air of Earth; the 'empty' space around us is 'filled' with meaning, each moment holds a universe of information in interpenetrating bondage. Because we cannot 'see' these 'other worlds' we do not for one moment believe that they don't exist.

The issue is one of access. To 'tune in' to any 'waveband' in the spectrum we need the right instrument, the right kind of 'eye'. This already reassures us that there must be realities beyond those our senses perceive. Most biologists accept that our present organs of perception are not, in any sense, 'perfected sensors'; rather, they are functions of the particular stage we have reached in our evolutionary development. The point of this is that evolution is an ongoing process; just as human eyes see 'better' than those of the more primitive tunicates which preceded us, so there is every reason to expect that future, more sophisticated eyes will see more, much more, than we see.

Will these future eyes be aspects of our biological being or might they utilise principles entirely different from those of optics? Here is where you may start to get some feeling for where we may be heading. It is significant to me that we already speak of a sense of symmetry to describe the conjunction of elements in our minds that has the capacity to appreciate rhythm. The great Yoga traditions of the East have understood for thousands of years that the *mind's eye* can be trained to access *non-ordinary realities* through what are now called *non-ordinary states of consciousness*, by which they mean levels that occupy positions in the rainbow of mind different from the ordinary waking consciousness in which most of us live out the uneventful working of an uneventful day.

So the problem becomes one of learning to 'tune in' to those aspects of the spectrum of reality that are currently 'invisible' to us. To do this we must investigate the mechanism of perception, seeking to know what consciousness is so we may see what it can become. For this I can say confidently: only when we truly understand the inner nature of thought itself can we find the holy grail of our shared searching, the deep answer to the deep question whose asking haunts this journey: *Who am I?*

Chapter 6

**thinking the
thought**

To grasp the essential nature of perception let us recap what
has been said about the quantum wave, the ripple of possibility.

· It does not exist in the time and space of ordinary experience.
· It encodes information.
· If you focus on one aspect of it (say position), other aspects
  (momentum) become fuzzy.
· It only becomes 'real' when you look at it.

Does this tug at your memory? Does it sound familiar? Could
you not say just the same things about a thought?

· A thought does not occupy time or space in the usual sense.
· It encodes information.
· If you focus on one thought, other thoughts blur.
· Thoughts only take on 'shape' when you concentrate on them,
  which is another way of saying that a thought only becomes
  'real' when you 'see' it in your mind.

Many physicists have sensed this similarity between quantum
ripples and thoughts. As David Bohm has aptly said:

We may well now ask whether the close analogy between
quantum processes and our inner experiences and thought processes
is mere coincidence . . . the remarkable point-by-point analogy
between thought processes and quantum processes would suggest
that a hypothesis relating these two may well turn out to be
fruitful.[57]

To take the next step in our journey we must abandon the
consensus view of science and explore not what science believes
to be true but what we intuit to be true. This is a big jump
to make. Earlier I spoke of 'truth' as often encoded in paradox.
In the same spirit of primal understanding I now want to suggest
to you that the human mind can often sense the *poetic* truth
of something long before science can affirm that truth in terms
of its own frames of reference. So when I say to you that
I believe thoughts are quantum ripples and quantum ripples
are thoughts, I am asking you to ignore the literal meaning
of my words and let your intuition resonate to the music of
a connection whose logic is not accessible by means of language.
Almost no physicist would go so far as to simply 'equate' ripples
of possibility and thoughts. And neither do I. What I am
suggesting—and it is vitally important—is that thought has
a quantum character so central to its essence that any future
physics of consciousness that is not rooted in quantum principles
must, from the perspective of a more enlightened knowing,
be false.[58]

A different way to approach this issue is to focus the 'lateral
thinking' technique on the process that makes it possible. Ask
yourself, 'What comes spontaneously to mind when you think
of thoughts?'. The answer is that we intuitively use wave-like
images when we describe our thought processes. For example,
when we identify with someone else's thinking, we often say
we are *in tune* with their mind or that we *resonate* with their
thoughts or that we are *on the same wavelength*. When someone
has a flash of insight we say they have had a *brainwave*.

Somehow, deep down, we have always known that thoughts
are ripples of possibility, waves, resonances, until they are made
'real' to others by an act of speech. Earlier, I likened the mind
to a pool of water and words to stones dropped into that
pool. And I said that what conveys meaning is not the stone
but the ripple it sends out. I suspect that 'resonated' with you;
you knew *that* it was true without knowing *why* it was true.

We can develop this further by considering what happens
during meditation. When someone goes into a proper
meditational state they lose all sense of that inner witness,
the self. The noise of confusing thoughts, the bustle of restless
mental activity finally fades away, leaving the pool of the mind
calm and still. No stones are being dropped into that pool,
no ideas are being processed. Is a person in such meditational
stillness conscious? Of course they are; they are in a state of
expanded consciousness, free of the distractions of sensory input.

Let me put this in more 'scientific' language. When there
is no sense of self, there is no mental 'observer' to observe,
so there is nothing in your mind to collapse the wave functions
of the quantum ripples that inhabit it; no ripples of possibility
are focused into 'realities'. Yet meditation does not obliterate
consciousness; rather, it heightens it.

What happens in deep meditation? Here is the crucial key.
For the last three chapters you may have noticed that I have
been using the words 'reality' and 'consciousness' almost
interchangeably. This is because, in the final analysis, reality
and consciousness are not separate. In deep meditation the
distinction vanishes, so that the seer is the seen, the thinker
is the thought. The great spiritual traditions have always
understood this.

The Nazarene, Jesus, captured the essence of it, in these words:

When you make the inner [thought] . . . as the outer
[physical], . . . then shall you enter the Kingdom [completed
understanding].[59]

The German mystic Meister Eckhart put it just as well when he said, simply:

The knower is the known.[60]

The Kalahari bushmen say it this way:

The dream is dreaming itself.[61]

A modern mystic, Krishnamurti, expressed the same insight with the words:

The thinker is the thought, the experiencer is the experienced.[62]

Indeed, Krishnamurti captured the essence of my argument:

Consciousness is its content.[63]

All this may sound strange so let me try and bring it to life in yet another way, using an example you can readily relate to. Imagine that you are suspended in the darkness of deep space. You are alone, in a situation where you cannot see any trace of your own body; you cannot feel, smell, taste or touch any aspect of your own physical structure. Your body, but not your mind, has been put to sleep so you cannot perform any action, you cannot speak, you cannot move, you cannot feel; you are effectively *disembodied*.

Focus on this strange state. Your deprivation is total; you have no sensation of anything—no sight, no sound, no movement—just the utter blackness of an absolute void. Now, in this disembodied state, isolated from all sensory input, *how do you know you are there at all?* The point of this parable is that, if I am right, your disembodied mind could not collapse the wave functions of anything outside itself, and quite possibly could not collapse any wave functions at all. Your thoughts would be just that—thoughts. Yet all my experience—and yours—tells us that you would still have consciousness. You would still be *real*.

You can see where my logic is heading. I am saying what Krishnamurti said, that consciousness is its content. Just that. You could counter—and quite rightly—that in meditation and in this imaginary state of sensory deprivation, the brain is still there, that consciousness can only exist because it is grounded in the ongoing activity of a living nervous system. This is the apparently unassailable position science holds. And with good reason, for all the evidence available to us suggests that consciousness is a direct function of the electrical circuitry of a living brain.

But is this true? Let us work through this. Your normal waking consciousness is characterised by several key elements:

- a sense of *self*—the feeling that you are the 'centre' of your world
- a sense of *linear time*—the feeling that time passes by in a regular sequence
- a sense of *separateness*—a feeling that you are a discrete atom of consciousness
- a fear of *death*.

Why has your consciousness taken on these qualities? Because your brain has evolved to maximise your chances of survival in a risky world. The tools of human awareness—your senses—have been trained by natural selection to focus on the 'here' in space and the 'now' in time, that is, to keep your mind concentrated on just those features of the environment that most affect your survival prospects. Your window to reality is a narrow sensory band that screens out most aspects of the world around you. Your brain is thus an extraordinarily effective filter whose prime function is not to expand your consciousness, but, in a very real sense, to *contract* it.

This has happened because a biological danger can only be avoided by biological action, which means realising a particular quantum possibility through the collapse of its associated wave function. So the brain has evolved a twofold role: (1) to sense the quantum ripples around it and (2) to trigger the collapse of selected wave functions of ripples in its immediate environment in both space and time. What else is your waking consciousness but the picture you create of your immediate surrounds? When you say 'I'm conscious that I'm in this room', you refer to the picture your brain is making of the things around you—the chairs, the vase of flowers and so on. When you say 'I'm conscious that it's two o'clock', you refer to the image your brain is making of the face of your watch, with its digital read-out.

What your brain is doing is filtering the vast input of quantum waves from the universe around you and, on the basis of past experience, picking those most relevant to where you are and when you are. But here is the point of my suggestion that these quantum waves have the essential character of thoughts. In effect, what I am saying is that *the whole quantum cosmos around you is conscious*—is latent consciousness in a universal sense—but that your brain restricts its 'field of awareness' only to what is important to you. Which is what its biology has trained it to do. Your brain is not the seat of your consciousness, as you always thought; rather, it is the guarding censor that, from the wider spectrum of awareness, selects only what impacts most strongly on your biological well-being.

This is a staggering turn-around. And its central message is—excuse the pun—mind-blowing. It is that deep consciousness, ongoing awareness, *does not depend on the brain for its existence*.

The botanist Rupert Sheldrake uses the following analogy.[64] Imagine an inquisitive extra-terrestrial that lands on earth and sees the moving technicolour image on a TV screen. Intrigued, it decides to find out where the picture is coming from. Like the good scientist it is, it takes the set apart, examines the wiring, analyses the cathodes and diodes and so on. But, of course, no matter how hard it tries, it cannot find the source of the picture inside the set because the image comes not from the set itself but from the electromagnetic field which fills the space around it. Sheldrake's point is that our brains are like the hardware of the TV set. Their function is to collect and focus the 'thought waves' around us and so 'paint a picture' in our minds of the resulting analysis—what we might call our 'picture of the world'. This means that the actual 'field of consciousness' our brains sample is already in existence all around us, as a matrix of quantum waves of possibility; this is the universal 'field' we enter during meditation or moments of mystical insight when our inner witness, our sense of self, fades away.

What then of the hard evidence that pegs consciousness to brain function? One example may suffice. When we faint we 'lose consciousness' and there can be no doubt that fainting is due to a reduced supply of blood to the brain. This seems to prove beyond all doubt that awareness is pegged—directly—to brain activity. If our quantum model of consciousness were correct it would mean that we would never 'lose' consciousness.

But let us think this through to its conclusion. When you sleep you dream, but when you wake up you forget what you have dreamt, unless you take the precaution of quickly writing down the main features of your dream before its image fades from your mind. Why do you forget? Because the brain's chief function is to ensure survival and your survival chances are best when you are most wide awake. So as soon as you wake up your brain is programmed to screen out all irrelevant inputs, including those arising from any non-ordinary state of consciousness, such as dreaming. In other words, you *do* remain conscious during the dreaming state (although your mind is tuned to a different 'frequency') but you do not remember your moments of dreaming consciousness in waking consciousness. To mix images from dreams with images from the world around you would be to jeopardise your chances of survival, to muddle your awareness of and reactions to opportunity and danger.

This is what happens when you faint. By definition, when you faint you become biologically helpless. So the moment you 'regain' consciousness your memories of what happened during the other-conscious state are wiped away so your brain, alert once more, can focus again on the 'here' of space and the 'now' of time. But the memories may still be there. People may later overcome their amnesia, they may remember some or all of what took place while they were 'blacked out'—days, weeks, months or even years after the episode.

My model of consciousness holds that it is impossible for deep awareness to disappear. What happens is that we remember only a tiny fraction of our past experiences at any one time because, in an important sense, almost all our past is not relevant to the imperatives of our present. Focus on your own impression of consciousness right now. What is your brain doing at this very moment? It is performing its prime function by filtering out the full richness of the awareness that surrounds it and keeping your mind focused only on what you are reading, thus cramping your awareness into this wafer-thin monolayer of reality we call this present moment and this shrunken circle of reality we call this present place.

Deep consciousness is *unbroken*. Night and day, waking and sleeping, winter and summer you are always conscious, on one level or another. Think back to the iron in your body that is, still, the star it came from. You are all you have been. Just as the continuity of your body is unbroken, one process, so even more the continuity of your consciousness is unbroken, one process.

This may sound radical but it is really an ancient insight. In the Buddhist tradition consciousness is eternal, it never vanishes. In the words of the Dalai Lama, 'deep mind [is] always there'.[65] There is no interruption to the continuity of deep consciousness, not even by death!

Chapter 7

---

realities we do not see

The preceding two chapters have developed the concept of a spectrum of consciousness without explaining what its component levels are. It is time now to explore this issue and to unscramble a source of confusion that confounds almost all attempts to make sense of something as intimate as the essence of what we are.

The metaphor of the rainbow of reality and the rainbow of consciousness I mapped out in Chapter 5 had the following 'wavebands':

low-frequency	physical reality	all sub-human states of consciousness
mid-frequency	mental/waking reality	ordinary human consciousness
high-frequency	imaginal/dreaming reality	symbolic and non-ordinary states of consciousness

all frequencies   unitary reality   no-boundary
                                                  consciousness

Let us start at the most obvious level, with the most familiar thing. What is physical consciousness? I have already hinted that it is a field of consciousness made up of those quantum ripples that embody 'physical' things. We access it through our biological senses and, from the inexhaustible field of its potential possibilities, we select those idiosyncratic elements that, jointly, make up our human picture of the world.

Now this physical picture is part of our waking consciousness but you will notice that the physical band is on a 'lower' plane than the waking band. Why? Here is where this journey of exploration will truly become a voyage of self-discovery, as I promised at the beginning of this book. Try this experiment. Take a good look at the wall in front of you, notice the pictures, where they are and what they are, notice the vase and the flowers it contains. Now close your eyes and visualise the wall as it would be if the position of the vase and the flowers were reversed. Can you see this revised image? Maybe not in such detail but you can see its broad outline. Why? You are not simply 'remembering' it, for you have changed its structure. What you are seeing is not the wall but the *mental image of it your mind is making.* Just as when you grope your way through your house at night, you know your way even though the lights are off. Why? Because your mind has made a model of your house. This mental model is no phantom, no will-o'-the-wisp of imagination, it is real enough to guide you in the absence of sensory input. You are back in that disembodied space we spoke of before, knowing a reality you cannot see.

Now carry the experiment further. Close your eyes again. Be aware of the room you are in and imagine that all noise has stopped. There are no sights, no sounds, no smells. Once you have got into the 'mood' of this you will cease to be aware of the seat you're sitting on. Now, in this real state of marked sensory deprivation work through an example of some simple mathematical operation like the equation $x = y^3 - z^2$. Let y equal 4 and z equal 3. What is the value of x? Do the calculation in your head.

You may find this easy but that is not the point. What I'm driving at is that you have, in your mind, manipulated symbols that in everyday reality are *not there* and you have come up with an answer that, in the physical world, *does not exist*. Do you begin to see where I am trying to take you? This mental world is *real* but it is *different*. It has its own logic, its own laws and—quite literally—its own is-ness. This is the field of *imaginal consciousness*, the world of images, symbols, ideas, metaphors, myths, archetypes. Like the field of physical consciousness, it exists all around you but you do not access it with the eyes of your head, rather with the 'eyes' of your mind. With your mind's eye. I describe this as a 'higher-frequency' state of consciousness because (so far as we know) only humans can access it. And because it does not inhabit the doomed prison of matter.

Poets and writers tend to have a better feel for the 'reality' of the imaginal field because they have direct experience of it. When they write 'creatively', they often report a certain astonishment. Where did the insights they have just captured in words come from? What was there in their prior experience that could have generated such wonderfully unexpected ideas? In terms of the explanation I am trying to develop, what is happening is that their minds are accessing the field of imaginal consciousness, which I see as the wellspring of human creativity.

An examination of the imaginal field shows why it is so attractive to postulate that thought is essentially quantum in nature. An alternative way to describe the quantum wave of an electron is to abandon the image of a 'ripple of possibility' and speak instead of a multi-layered composite of dreamlike *virtual* states. In terms of this imagery, an unobserved electron exists as an infinity of superposed virtual 'fantasies'. The act

of seeing selects a particular state from the infinite dream display
and collapses its wave function into a discrete 'reality'. Notice
how this description mimics the act of creative imagination.
When we want to 'create' a story or a poem or an idea, we
'daydream'; that is, we 'open our minds' to the inexhaustible
spectrum of virtual (imaginal) possibilities that hover like
phantoms on the edge of reality. So it is easy to believe that
when we 'zoom in' on an idea by picking an option from
the field of imaginal possibility we collapse the wave function
of the associated imaginal state; so that what was an unfocused
'dream' becomes a focused concept; this, I submit, is how the
creative act happens.

Einstein once said that 'imagination is more important than
knowledge'. One can say to oneself, 'Tonight I will read a
chapter of this textbook' and do it. But one cannot say to
oneself, 'Tonight I will create a great poem'. Inspiration comes
in its own time, when the mind is ready, or it comes not at
all. There is a freakishness, an unpredictability, about insight
that makes it impossible to pin down. Why? Because the mind
has to become receptive to the depth of the imaginal field in
order to access insight; it has to 'tune in' to the right
'wavelength'. This process is not under our 'conscious' control
because it is a function of what we are, not what we do.

Consider those 'Eureka' moments of insight that have
empowered the scientific quest. One well-documented case is
that of the French mathematician Poincaré, who was wrestling
with a particular mathematical problem that he was unable
to solve by deliberate reasoning. Frustrated, he decided to go
for a bus ride.

At the moment when I put my foot on the step, the idea came to
me, without anything in my former thoughts seeming to have
paved the way for it, that the transformations I had used to define
Fuchsian functions were identical with those of non-Euclidian
geometry. I did not verify the idea; I should not have had time, as

upon taking my seat in the omnibus, I went on with a
conversation already commenced, but I felt a perfect certainty.[66]

The 'all-at-onceness' that is a characteristic feature of
scientific insight also fires artistic inspiration. Read Mozart's
description of how he composed his works:

Then my soul is on fire with inspiration. The work grows; I keep
expanding it, conceiving it more and more clearly until I have the
entire composition finished in my head though it may be long.
Then my mind seizes it as a glance of my eye a beautiful picture or
a handsome youth. It does not come to me successively, with
various parts worked out in detail, as they will later on, but in its
entirety that my imagination lets me hear it.[67]

My quantum description gives all thoughts a wave character.
In terms of the musical metaphor that structures this text,
insights like those above can be described as occasions when
the wave functions of hitherto separate notes suddenly *vibrate
in tune*, when chords which are discordant when separate
suddenly meld into a pattern of harmonically combined 'standing
waves'.[68] Notice how insights, unlike processes of reasoning,
are invariably both non-linear and non-verbal. Nothing is
collapsed into 'sharp-edged' words that are structured in a this-
after-that manner; rather, the 'Eureka' insight is typically a
magic instant of knowing. Indeed, both Mozart and Poincaré
stress that it may take hours to set down in linear, scripted
form the fullness of the understanding that came to them in
that one intuitive moment of revelation. This kind of *globality*
is characteristic of quantum processes and it makes sense in
view of the wave nature of thought.

The imaginal realm resembles what the Swiss psychologist
Carl Jung dubbed the realm of the *collective unconscious*. The
term 'unconscious' is unfortunate since it suggests a world
somehow lurking 'below' the level of waking consciousness,

whereas the imaginal realm is actually 'higher' in the rainbow of consciousness; it is the font of deep insight, the taproot of intuition, the pointer not to the past but the future.

Many people will want to ask, 'If this imaginal field is actually "out there" why do we only access it in moments of insight? Why can't we access it directly, at will? Why can't our mind's eye make a world from it?'. But—and here is my whole point—we can, we do. *Where do you think your thoughts come from?*

It is critical that this idea is understood. Many, probably most, of the thoughts we experience are those we 'tune into' in the field of imaginal possibility around us. *They are already there.* When we concentrate on a problem, our mind's eye samples the thought field around it and selects, within the limitations of its ability, the images or symbols most relevant to its searching. We think we have created them when, in truth, we have merely captured them. Watch the images that appear on a computer screen, as you type out the words of a poem. Or a story. Or an essay. Are those words, those ideas, becoming real only as they appear on the screen? Are they not real in the mind that makes them? Or finds them? I would say that what you are doing with the computer is projecting into the realm of physical reality formed images that have their origin in imaginal reality.

But this does not mean they have always been there. For each present thought there was a moment of prior creation that had its genesis in a human mind. Human minds cannot create the thoughts that made flowers or bees or weasels; they already exist in the possibility field of physical reality. But they can create the ideas that inhabit our mental universe, they can weave the rich loom of human symbolism. And these imaginal thoughts, born of us, are as real as the quantum ripples that make up an electron. Or an atom. Or a rock.

This creative process is an ongoing and pivotal feature of human evolution. During the course of your life you may create several radically new thoughts that never existed before. They will be your 'brain-children'. Quite literally! And these children of your insight can outlast the brain that created them. As Mary Renault has written, hauntingly: 'The sons of dreams outlive the sons of seed'.[69]

This is the strange reality—all thoughts, whatever 'waveband' they occupy, exist in the disembodied reality of the quantum dream. The essence of a quantum ripple is that it exists in an indeterminate, non-localised state, in that uninhabited quantum 'space' where there is neither yesterday nor tomorrow, neither here nor there. Moreover, a thought, once created, no longer needs the physical structure of the brain that made it to sustain it further—it is thereafter just as 'real' as an electron or a stone.

Common sense tends to rebel at this. We have such an ingrained tendency to explain aspects of experience in terms of everyday models that our minds stumble when confronted with a phenomenon for which there is no model. But the quantum state poses the ultimate paradox: it seems so alien because it is so familiar. Our thoughts are, in essence, quantum waves so when we see this inner aspect of ourselves in outward projection we think we are seeing the face of a stranger. The nub of the difficulty is the disembodied aspect of the quantum ripple. Because the world we inhabit is limited by the dimensional context of space and time, it is difficult for our minds to grasp the dimensionless reality of the thoughts that enter them.

The best way to resolve one paradox is to invoke another so let me sketch out a further anti-intuitive aspect of quantum mechanics. Consider two subatomic particles, A and B, that are created from the same micro-event in such a way that A has a different 'spin' to B. Suppose further that these two particles now proceed to opposite 'ends' of the universe. They are so far apart that a signal travelling at the speed of light could not bridge the gap between them. The mind-bending scientific truth is that if one changes the spin on A, the spin on B changes simultaneously. Since no signal can travel faster than light we are obviously dealing with a coupled system that cannot obey the spacetime logic we recognise. This paradoxical non-locality of quantum interactions means that even though human observers measure the space (or time) between the particles in terms of the millions of kilometres (or years) that (seem to) separate them, at a deeper level of reality they are still—somehow—together. So any point we call 'here' can simultaneously access all of space in exactly the same sense that, as the mystics assure us, any moment we call 'now' can simultaneously access all of time.

Mathematical theorist Rudy Rucker believes that mathematical truths occupy a 'mental space' which he dubs the Mindscape. 'A person who does mathematical research,' he opines, 'is an explorer of the Mindscape in much the same way that Armstrong, Livingstone or Cousteau are explorers of the physical features of our universe.'[70] Other scientists seem to agree. Roger Penrose states:

> When mathematicians communicate, this is made possible by each one having a *direct route to truth* [author emphasis], the consciousness of each being in a position to perceive mathematical truths directly, through this process of 'seeing'.[71]

While evidently keeping his options open on this issue, Paul Davies cites some powerful arguments in its favour. He writes of several mathematical geniuses who have had the ability to write theorems down without going through the processes of logical 'proof' normally required in such cases. Arguably the most famous case is that of Srinivasa Ramanujan. Born of a poor family in India and with limited education, he more or less taught himself what little formal maths he knew. From this unpromising start he went on to write down, without proof, a veritable treasurehouse of mathematical theorems and conjectures, many of which were subsequently 'proved' by

Western mathematicians while others still defeat all attempts to decipher their meaning. Davies homes in on the extraordinary feature of this:

> We are, of course, used to the fact that all human abilities,
> physical and mental, show wide variations. Some people can jump
> six feet off the ground, whereas most of us can manage barely
> three. But imagine someone coming along and jumping sixty feet,
> or six hundred feet! Yet the intellectual leap represented by
> mathematical genius is far in excess of these physical differences.[72]

Davies' conclusion? 'It is very tempting to suppose that Ramanujan had a particular faculty that enabled him to view the mathematical Mindscape directly and vividly, and pluck out ready-made results at will'.

Another example that strongly supports the reality of the Mindscape is the famous Mandelbrot set[73] with its strangely symmetric whorls and tendrils. It is impossible to believe that Mandelbrot 'created' this aspect of chaos theory: in some veritable sense the set was already there before he 'found' it.[74] Which brings us to the special relevance of this example. Where was it? Or rather, where is it? The Mandelbrot set, like any element of the mathematical Mindscape, cannot exist in ordinary space and time since minds at any point on the earth's surface have equal access to it. It is tempting to speculate that the Mindscape is quantum in character and that its universal accessibility reflects the holistic qualities of quantum systems, as exemplified in the non-local effects previously discussed.

Thus far, the concept of the Mindscape has been restricted to mathematical 'truths' because it is comparatively easy to ascribe an independent reality to concepts which are universally the same for all who find and use them. But, once the idea of a Mindscape is allowed, it is difficult to see any a priori reason why it should not be generalised to include all the symbolic elements that inhabit the cognitive world of human thought. In this sense the Mindscape can be seen as a special (unchanging) sub-set of the (changing) imaginal realm.

The physical landscape seems more reliably 'real' and 'solid' than the imaginal Mindscape because all normal human beings access 'physical' quantum consciousness in a similar way. Those quantum 'thoughts' (collapsed into physical tangibility) have been 'real' for tens of millions or thousands of millions, or millions of millions of years, depending on how 'old' the physical 'idea' they embody is in evolutionary terms, so there is a staunchly supported consensus 'pattern' to the world they build.[75] By contrast, the imaginal field is, in evolutionary terms, only a few tens of thousands of years old. Its structure is still plastic, still forming, not fixed. It is, in a deep sense, evolving too quickly to have taken shape. So different minds sample different elements of it. Few minds as yet create the same world from it and there is no unanimity as to what the final 'form' of this reality will be.

The concept of multiple realities is alien to most people so let me give you one last example before we move on. Suppose your senses could pick up all the 008-accessed messages that fill the air around you, what would happen? Yes, you would go crazy. Your mind would be bombarded with information from all directions at once and, since your brain does not have sufficient parallel processing capacity, you would not be able to build a coherent picture of your world. To avoid this information overload, your brain has had to develop an efficient discriminatory filter which screens out the whole reality spectrum except for the one tiny slit which is the focus of its concentration; this gives you directional (eyes front) access to a very limited input in a serial (one-after-the-other) fashion.

Think of the different ways you experience your world. When you are searching intently for something, an exercise book or a lost item of clothing, you are focused on your physical surroundings so your mind is predominantly tuned to the physical waveband that is the immediate focus of its attention. When you sit at your desk and daydream, you tend to filter out awareness of your physical situation and your mind's eye can access the imaginal field. This is always the prerequisite to entry into other states of consciousness—that your physical body is still and safe so your mind is for the moment relieved of the need to monitor the environment around it for opportunity or danger. This is what happens during sleep for in sleep your brain enters a different state of receptiveness that is wholly open to the imaginal frequency. Perhaps this is why sleep evolved among animals, to create a space where their minds could begin to tap into other realities, to dimly know other states of consciousness, to dream dreams.

Meditation offers the best window of all. Before you meditate you always make sure you are in a quiet spot, away from all distracting inputs. Then, over time, you learn to let go of all the models your brain has created to make sense of its world. Until, at its limit, your mind becomes open to the whole spectrum of reality that surrounds it, knowing it without processing it.

So the consciousness we thought so simple is really a multi-layered thing. There is waking consciousness and there is dreaming consciousness and there are tantalising glimpses of other states of consciousness that come to us so fleetingly during gaps in our concentration, in the silence between the sounds. Which brings us to the very nub of the problem, the box that remains when its wrappings have gone.

Chapter 8

knowing the
magic key

We now come to the central message of this book, we arrive at the place we have for so long sought to find; the indestructible centre that is left when the last wrapping has been removed from the box of truth. It is time to bring in the last actor in the cast, your mind's 'I', your *sense of self*.

As promised in the introduction, I have tried to make this book as experiential as possible; I have tried to involve you, the reader, at every stage in the development of my thesis. We now come to the point where we deal with the very essence of what we are. So to get into the point at issue, focus on this moment of 'now' that is the only reality you currently inhabit. And ask yourself this simple question: What is happening in this present moment that allows me to be conscious of it?

My answer is this; your mind makes this moment on the basis of its memories, which allow it to order its sensory input so as to make a coherent picture. This much is certain, when you open your eyes as a newborn babe all you see is an unstructured fuzz. You have to *learn* to see, by learning to measure the length of an object by means of the shadow its edges cast, computing distance by the perspective-structured relationship between objects, and so on. It is this computational 'software' in your brain that enables you to 'put it all together', to make sense of what you see.

Why am I stressing the pattern of this seeing? Quite simply because the fundamental act of seeing is an act of *integration*. This is almost the last link in the chain, the key insight; *the integrative act of consciousness is the act of knowing.*

Let me focus this idea more sharply. If you did not recognise the whole intricate web of relationships in your field of vision as an *orderly* pattern you would not see at all. The very word 'recognise' means 'know again', implying that what you know now you have, somewhere and somewhen, known before. This is obvious if you think about it; if the pattern of one moment differed from the pattern of its predecessor by too big a margin you would not recognise it, there would be an interruption in the continuity of consciousness, resulting in a disorientation so severe it would quite literally fracture being.

Why is this important? Because we are talking about your very essence, the you that you feel yourself to be. What is your self-consciousness of this moment but your knowing of it, and what is your knowing of it but the way you integrate the input of experience, *to make sense of your world*?

But we are still skating on the surface, we are still speaking of the 'you' that is the you of this moment and so we are missing the whole point! Up to now we have described consciousness only in terms of the picture it paints in your mind at any given instant. But on its own this picture is nothing; it is a 'surface without substance', a layer without depth. Where does that depth come from? It comes from *time*. What has been missing from our discussion of consciousness so far is the *depth* that time introduces. This present moment of consciousness is only made possible by all its past moments of consciousness; the act of present seeing is made possible by all those acts of past seeing that enable the present sight to be known for what it is. This is the deeper meaning of what I said earlier: *you still are all you once were.*

Whenever in this book I have used the term 'deep', I have been referring to the topic under discussion in terms of its *depth in time.* Thus deep consciousness means consciousness stretched out along the dimension of time. So the you of the moment is the surface you; the 'deep you' which is the 'real you', is the self that has this depth in time. This deep knowing is unique to you and, at the same time, accessible to all other minds whose sensors are similarly 'tuned'. What Jung called the 'collective unconscious' might be better described as the *collective knowing* of the human species. The imaginal realm of reality is not merely the source of the symbols and archetypes humans have created down the ages; it is *the knowing that integrates them*—into myths, stories, theories, epics, poems. Without these linking threads the imaginal field would simply be a soup of unconnected 'ideas'.

All human beings are born with the same sensory equipment so the physical reality they see is the same. This is why the physical level seems so tangible—everyone can access it. But human beings differ chaotically in the degree of development of the 'inner eye' by which they access the changing flux of imaginal reality. So this level seems flimsy, will-o'-the-wisp, unreal. But links do exist. How often have you thought of someone at the very moment the phone rings and that person says they have just thought of you. These 'synchronicities' are shared tappings of the imaginal code.

When you access imaginal reality you may capture individual images, individual thoughts, but you may also tap into the evolving matrix of knowing that unites them in an ever-changing adventure. When you extract a deep insight from imaginal consciousness you may be capturing the depth of an integration some prior mind has already performed. But the pattern you make in your mind, using this 'revelation', will be different again. It, too, will become part of the collective knowing, a knowing that evolves as it grows.

How does it evolve, how do you grow in knowing? The obvious answer is that information is conveyed by words. A teacher explains how to do simultaneous equations, he draws examples on the board and the class 'understands' the principle. So there is apparently a straightforward transfer of knowing, with words acting as vehicles to carry the message:

teacher's mind   →   words/examples   →   pupils' mind.

But does it happen like this? No, of course not. The teacher can spell out the message over and over again but if the pupil's mind is not ready the exchange of knowing will not take place. Remember the metaphor I used earlier? What conveys meaning is not the word but the ripple it sends out. The knowing is in the ripple, not the word, and the 'waves' in the 'water' of the pupil's mind must resonate with the wave form of the message to 'take it in'. Only then does the pupil experience that 'aha' moment of insight, of understanding, of integration.

Indeed the process set out above is, in my view, both wrong and misleading. A more accurate representation might be as follows:

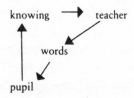

In other words, the pupil accesses the knowing *directly*, the teacher's words acting merely as cues or prompts.[76] In fable form you can imagine the knowing shining with the light of truth. The teacher's mind has already seen that shining. What he does with words is hold up a mirror so the light is directed towards the pupil, who will only 'see the light' if the mirror is angled the right way. After which she sees the light herself.

There is an explosive concept hidden in this seemingly innocuous statement. To see what it is, let us tease out the basic structure of the act of knowing. In my view, consciousness of any kind—physical, waking, imaginal—is a matrix of uncollapsed quantum waves, thoughts, as we have been discussing in the past few chapters. Up to now we have proceeded on the assumption that the only way to access these 'thought-fields' is to collapse the wave function of the relevant quantum ripple, yielding a 'sharp-edged' thing—a word or a particle. Now I propose something radically different. I propose that, provided your mind is in the right 'state', the right mode, you can access reality *by resonance alone*.

This is a truly deep insight. And it is the freshest, the most original insight I can give you. Let me repeat it, quietly. *It is only when subject and object remain in wave form that the transfer of knowing can take place.*

Up to now we have assumed that the only way to accesss any waveband of reality is to collapse the wave function of the associated 'thought'. What I am now saying is that there is another way—the way of knowing which links our minds directly to the object of our thoughts by melding the selected quantum wave form of our 'thoughts' with the selected quantum wave form of the 'entity' on which we focus, *without collapsing the wave of either.*

This concept is difficult but central. So let me tease out its meaning. The act of observation creates 'sharp-edged' realities—particles or words—but these creations are not knowings. You are conscious of the 'physical' reality of created things but you are not conscious of the knowing that unites them. You can demonstrate the 'non-collapsible' quality of knowing to yourself quite simply. Think of the mathematical symbol 'x' and you will see an image shaped like two crossed sticks. This image is an item drawn from the imaginal field and formed by the collapse of its associated wave function. But try to visualise the *understanding* that lets you solve for 'x' in a quadratic equation. Can you? No, you can't. Why? Because this knowing, like all knowing, does not have 'shape' although it does have 'structure'; it is the resonance energy of connected, in-phase 'thoughts'. And while you can 'image' the component thoughts you can't image the resonance between them.

When you 'resonate' with someone or intuit something, your mind links with that thing or that person by way of cohering wave functions without collapsing the wave in any way. When this happens you *become* the object of your 'seeing'. Remember? The seer *becomes* the sight, the knower the known, the thinker the thought, as the mystics have always claimed. This coupling is the coherent reinforcement of in-phase wave patterns: on the one side the quantum thoughts in the seer's mind, on the other the quantum thoughts that define the object or person who is the focus of that mind.

In the Introduction I quoted T.S. Eliot:

We shall not cease from exploration
and the end of all our exploring
will be to arrive where we started
and know the place for the first time.

At that time I said that we all 'recognise' something in the lines without being able to express it in words. This is a good example of wave resonance. The recognition *is* the resonance; the inability to express it verbally is a sign that none of the associated wave functions have been collapsed into 'sound particles'.

The wave nature of the processes the brain uses to drive its activity can be demonstrated experimentally. The French mathematician B.J. Fourier developed a form of calculus that enables patterns to be converted into waves and vice versa.

Such conversions are called, appropriately, 'Fourier transforms'. When scientists applied this knowledge to the way the human eye functions they were able to show that the brain cells in the visual cortex (the part of the brain that decodes input from the eyes) responded not to the pattern of any given visual image but to the Fourier transform of the image.[77] *The intrinsic language of the brain is the language of wave forms.*[78]

This is the crux of my argument. *The integrative dynamics of thought are based entirely on uncollapsed wave functions.* This insight allows us to begin to understand how 'thought' works. Wave forms tend to sort themselves out according to their frequencies and patterns. So 'thought waves' always seek other waves of a similar resonance because only waves that are sufficiently in tune can link together in a meaningful way. When two people communicate verbally, the words they speak 'drop stones into the pond' and the resulting waves participate in a kind of frequency-driven 'computer search' for matching waves modulated in a compatible way. Knowing is an integrative process precisely because it obeys this universal hunger of all things, wave or particle, to come together, *to again be one*.

This new image of knowing has profound implications for our understanding of reality. The thesis I have been developing is that knowing is defined by integration. So knowing is the resonant integration of 'spread-out' thought waves that never fall into the traps of 'sharp-edged' matter or language. This has the truly profound implication that *knowing remains forever in wave form* which means it lives, in an important sense, outside normal space and time in the non-ordinary reality of the quantum wave state.

Another example may help. Think of a symphony. A broadcast symphony exists as a modulated set of finely integrated radio waves. Like light, radio waves are electromagnetic waves and, like light, they are from their own perspective timeless. A disembodied mind riding a radio wave would not experience any sense of linear time (remember Goethe's lines?).

Radio waves resemble quantum waves in key aspects of their character: they are *time-symmetric*—the equations that describe them have no inbuilt 'arrow of time' (in the universe as we know it radio waves seem to travel only from past to future but they are theoretically equally capable of moving in the opposite time direction)—and electromagnetic waves and quantum waves both *propagate of themselves*, they do not need a supporting medium, unlike sound which only travels through air. Indeed I have already indicated that the maths which describe a single radio wave 'quantum' are identical to the maths which describe a quantum wave proper, suggesting that there is a deep similarity between the two.[79]

In Chapter 4 we examined the dual nature of matter at its most elemental level, that of a single electron. We can now generalise and acknowledge that the whole of 'reality' has two aspects, a wave aspect and a particle aspect. While these two aspects are indissolubly coupled it is also true that waves and particles exhibit completely different kinds of behaviour. When a particle encounters a solid barrier it is often deflected or even destroyed, but a wave can 'bend around' the obstacle and even propagate beyond it. A large moving particle like a golf ball can smash a sheet of glass to pieces whereas a beam of light waves will pass harmlessly through it. Significantly, when information exists in particle form it cannot reach the speed of light whereas information encoded in any electromagnetic wave, by definition, travels at the speed of light.

The speed of light occupies a hinge position in the structure of reality. The term 'speed' is unfortunate as speed is so strongly associated with the idea of rapid motion. But the earth is moving at a phenomenal speed at this very moment and we don't feel it. It took the genius of Newton to recognise that we cannot tell whether a body is at rest (not moving) or moving uniformly in a straight line unless we have some external frame of reference to go by. It is only when a body changes direction that we become conscious of its motion. So the speed of light should be thought of less as a movement than as a threshold; it represents the dividing line between the world of particles and the world of waves. All real entities have a quantum wave structure: below light speed they can express themselves as particles whereas at or above light speed they must remain as waves.

So we now arrive at a concept which is as simple as it is awesome; *when reality exists in wave form it is not stringently subject to the 'here and now' space and time limitations that constrain ordinary particle-based matter.* And knowing, by its very nature, exists in wave form! This is why poetry is more evocative than prose—it is already partly cast in song and song has a wave structure. Music is the most alchemic force of all, for the resonances it sets up can vibrate in tune with the inner logic of the universe. This is because the universe is rhythmic at root, the ripples of possibility that constitute its rainbow of reality all exist in the musical wave form of the quantum state.[80]

When a wave pulse propagates it leaves behind a ripple of identical crests and troughs. Note the repetitive character of this 'harmonic'; this is why ancient forms of music—drummings or chantings—which have a strong reiterative flavour, are so effective in creating altered states of consciousness (Figure 6). When you get caught up in this hypnotic kind of music you will sometimes sway 'in tune' with its rhythm as your body unconsciously strives to express the song it senses.

There is a kind of music which is heard so deeply that it ceases to be heard at all. You yourself become the tune.[81]

The way we describe music reveals the reason why it has the effects it does. We call a powerful piece of music a *moving* composition, we speak of a song's ability to *sway* us. This shows that our natural response to good music is to move ourselves, which is why the word 'melody' comes from the Greek root-word 'melos' meaning 'limb'. And what happens

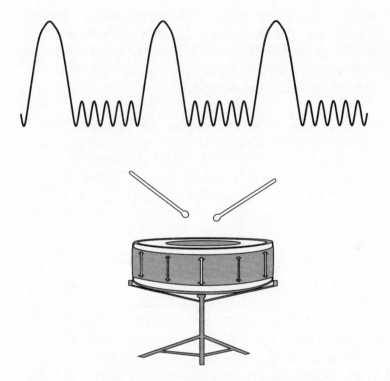

Figure 6 The repetitive trace of a drumbeat. Reiterative music like this can induce altered states of consciousness.

when we move ourselves in tune with music? Yes, we dance. This is what dance is, an attempt to weave a melody of movement, to make our bodies *become* the ecstasy of the song that stirs them. Thus was dancing born in olden times, as a sacred ritual to make manifest in movement the mystery of the world's unfolding.

Nature is (almost) always symmetrical so if reality has a fundamentally musical structure then music should highlight a deep relationship to reality. This means that, under the right circumstances, we should be able to reverse the relationship, that is, we should be able to start with music and end with matter, we should be able to make reality by singing (dancing) it into being. The Aborigines of Australia have understood for at least 40 000 years that song plays an important role in the relationship between seer and sight. As one white man who understands their Dreaming reports it:

> We start with nothing—a total emptiness—a void. Then we have
> some singing and dancing. We start by forming—the singing
> creates the sound and the vibration forms a shape, and the dancing
> helps solidify it. The dancing is making the form stand out as a
> tree, a bird, as land. The process, the Dreaming itself, becomes a
> reality, something we can work with and see.[82]

What does this mean? Simply said, a song played suitably on the imaginal waveband can set up matching ripples in the medium of the physical waveband which is on a lower level on the reality scale. It is a bit like plucking the high-pitched strings of a cello so the bass notes will vibrate 'in tune'.

Sometimes, during a peak experience or in meditation, a song can be simply transferred from one waveband to another if the 'frequencies' are adjusted with exacting precision. But there is another outcome, one which entails a more awesome consequence. If the 'pitch' of the singing is right, the upper-level singing can set up unstable vibrations in the lower-level medium. When this happens the lower-energy waves may not be able to absorb the more intense energy from the higher waveband, so the matching resonance that is set up in the lower waveband can lose its wave form altogether. In this situation it 'breaks up' in much the same way that a wine glass will shatter when a soprano's voice reaches a certain pitch.

What happens? The destabilised wave form implodes, *the wave function collapses*. Does that sound familiar? Perhaps this is how singings in the 'inner' world of mind affect structure in the 'outer' world of matter. At the very least this metaphor may help us see just what happens at that critical interface between observer and observed, seer and sight. Any act of seeing is an act of *recognition*, of seeing a second time what one has seen before. Re-cognition is the setting up of a re-sonance between two timeframes of the same image. So what happens in the act of recognition may be that imaginal knowing transmits a resonance pattern to the lower physical waveband, and if it is not stable in that waveband it causes the pattern to 'fall' out of the symmetrical world of waves into the one-way world of particles. During this transfer process the form of the singing changes (waves become particles) but its meaning (content) does not.

Thus an imaginal song may become a physical structure, the 'lower-energy' knowing may remake the higher in its own image. Almost literally. So, at its limit and under the right conditions, *knowing may create a world*, just as the Aborigines have said.

Knowing is therefore a kind of 'meta-reality'—a *reality behind reality*. The point I want to emphasise is that knowing has an existence, just like a rock or a buttercup. But it lives outside the doomed world of matter as a timeless music of cohering quantum ripples, a kind of self-sealing standing wave, a self-sustaining song, which is why it underpins the melodic structure of the *one song*, the *uni-verse*, which is *the harmonic summation of all that is*.

This is arguably the most difficult concept in this book. Throughout the text we have been talking about reality in one way or another but habit is a powerful force so our minds tend to stay stuck in the grooves they are comfortable with. This means we keep on thinking that the familiar reality we make from the physical waveband of consciousness is the *only* reality. We may be intellectually prepared to concede that the imaginal waveband has a reality of sorts but we still distrust it. With this sort of mindset it is extraordinarily difficult to endow an abstract concept like 'knowing' with any kind of *per se* reality at all, even when we specify that *knowing is the organised software of consciousness itself*.

As always in this kind of situation I will fall back on paradox; the best way to try and escape from an habitual mindset is to stay within it. So let us focus on the familiar field of physical consciousness and ask, 'What organises this field?'. The scientist's logical answer is 'the laws of physics'. In my symbolism these laws are a deep knowing because they integrate the phenomena that make up the world, they structure physical reality. If we now ask, 'Are these laws real?' we must answer, 'Of course they are'. The material universe would not exist without them! They are every bit as real as the particles whose motions they guide. They are the theme to whose music the particles dance.

These are new ideas and we need new words to describe them. How can we describe 'the organised structure of deep knowing'— the integrated music of knowing that stretches across time? The Aborigines have a beautiful expression which I can adapt to capture the flavour of my meaning; they use the term 'songlines' to describe the interwoven pattern of time-tracks that criss-cross the landscape of their land.[83]

Songlines.

This is the term I will use henceforth as an acceptable alternative for the problematic word 'soul'. I have said that an atom of iron is not a point but a line. Just so, a songline is the fullness of knowing over time.

So finally we arrive. Over and over again during our exploration of consciousness, in one way or another, we have been asking the oldest and most poignant of all questions: 'Who am I?'. I can now give you my answer:

We are the songlines of our lives.

Do you see the force of that? Do you see where all this has been leading inch by inch, since our minds first came into contact? If we are the songlines of our lives and if songlines know reality through resonance, then we must remain conscious *even after death*.

Chapter 9

---

the dark portal

We now approach a place of shadows we are afraid to enter. Death is the mystery we most fear, the terror we most dread. In Shakespeare's chilling words:

> Ay, but to die, and go we know not where . . .
> The weariest and most loathed worldly life
> that age, ache, penury, and imprisonment
> can lay on nature is a paradise
> to what we fear of death.[84]

I do not know how, or with what composure I will meet my own death but I have loved since boyhood a poem by Robert Browning:

> Fear death?—to feel the fog in my throat,
> the mist in my face,
> when the snows begin, and the blasts denote
> I am nearing the place,
> the power of the night, the press of the storm,
> the post of the foe;

where he stands, the Arch Fear in a visible form,
yet the strong man must go . . .[85]

Yet the strong man must go. Earlier I spoke of the quest for knowing as 'the hero's journey'. Death is the climax of this journey, the end of the path we have been following, the destination we reach at the conclusion of the voyage into ourselves. It is also the crisis that the voyage makes inevitable. For death is not only the last mystery, it is also the greatest challenge, the riskiest adventure, the final test. In Browning's words:

For the journey is done and the summit attained,
and the barriers fall,
though a battle's to fight ere the guerdon be gained,
the reward of it all.
I was ever a fighter, so—one fight more,
the best and the last!
I would hate that death bandaged my eyes, and forebore,
and bade me creep past.

Taking steel from Browning's courage, I am now going to invite you to overcome the denial of death that is such a persistent and pathological feature of our Western culture and look through the dark portal. I do not pretend that this will be an easy thing to do. In this forbidden kingdom, each step we take will be haunted by the demons of our darkest fears and lit by the longing of our brightest hopes. Our yearning is to see the vision splendid, the radiant triumph of love made manifest. Our terror is to discover nothing, not even night, only the bland vacuum of the spirit's absence. And we have a premonition of the precipice that may await us in a world of dreams, for where there are dreams there can also be nightmares. '. . . in that sleep of death what dreams may come when we have shuffled off this mortal coil?'[86]

I am not deploying these words for mere literary effect. In my understanding there *is* something here to fear. Earlier I spoke of the price tag all knowledge carries. In the case of death the price we must all pay for understanding is simply this, that what we discover we will remember. *What we come to know we must go on knowing.* I also have a another caution. On this last step of the journey we will find ourselves alone, as all humans are when they confront root issues they can only know through their own searching. So while I can and will use the insights of science to guide our path, I can't and don't claim to speak on behalf of science. That would be a lie.

Now let us approach this mystery called death. We have built up to this climax, step by step, during the course of our time together. And here are the roadmarks we have passed on our journey, the insights that make this moment possible:

1 Our sense of the passage of time is an illusion impressed upon us by the serial way we structure the symbolic flux of our thoughts.
2 In the perspective of relativistic physics, spacetime (the universe) simply is; there is no false division into past, present and future.
3 Each field of consciousness can be envisaged as a field of possibility made up of quantum 'thoughts'.
4 The function of the brain is to sample these fields for those aspects that most affect its survival prospects, which means restricting consciousness to the point in space we call 'here' and the moment in time we call 'now'.
5 Quantum thoughts are knit together by the integrative act of knowing that brings them into 'resonance'. This resonance is a function of the wave form of thoughts. Knowing structures quantum 'fuzz' into organised 'software'.

The key to understanding death is the insight we developed concerning the wave nature of resonant interaction. While we are alive, our biological brains access reality by resolving composite quantum waves into particulate realities, for all biological brains are locked into the feedback loop that requires them to monitor consciousness to enhance survival. When the brain dies, so does its ability to create a world by 'collapsing the wave functions' of the quantum ripples that influence it. But the songline of its consciousness accesses quantum fields not by collapsing wave functions but by resonance, and resonance is a phenomenon obeying different laws and creating different outcomes.

This is a hinge point of this text, so let me expand on it. We know the world by collapsing the multi-valent wave functions of the fields around us into things with 'edges'— particles or words. So strong, so tenacious, so seemingly universal is this impulse that we even erect an 'edge' around our psyches, calling the enclosed entity which results a 'self'. So the characteristic and defining feature of this familiar mode of access is the creation of boundaries. But resonance, which is the complementary mechanism, acts in a way that is symmetrically opposite. Its function is the *elimination* of boundaries because it brings the wave forms it integrates into direct union. It results in a loss of 'edges' leading, in the case of cognitive awareness, to the dissolution of the sense of 'self'.

Although it is not widely recognised, science has always acknowledged that, in a very real sense, 'we' continue to exist after death.[87] As we go through life we trace out a spacetime trajectory which is dubbed, in the parlance of physics, the *worldline* of our lives. This worldline is indissolubly part of the spacetime context in which it operated and it remains after our deaths as a 'locked-in contributor' to the ongoing integrity of the physical universe. Remember the exercise in Chapter 2 of going back to an experience you enjoyed? The point of that exercise was the lesson it made about the reality of the past; that the moment you enjoyed is *still there*, even though you can no longer access it. In just this sense, *the whole of your life is still there after you have died.*

Just as the worldline of our lives remains after death, so does the songline of its consciousness, and this songline, which is an integrated wave 'harmonic', accesses its reality in the all-at-once way of insight (remember Mozart's words?). Its knowing has the non-local *globality* of quantum wave phenomena, or to put it more impactively, it does not inhabit the linear flux of our time-structured experience since its essence is the time-free 'now' of integrated insight.

We *are* our knowing. What happens when we die is that we change the way we access consciousness: we cease to make a 'picture' of the world, we begin to know the 'essence' of the world; we no longer collapse the wave functions of our thoughts, we vibrate in tune with the singing that they sing. Notes will only vibrate in tune if they vibrate simultaneously so, in a profound sense, the one song of the uni-verse only exists because the wave forms of its varied notes are harmonically combined in the same 'timeless' structure which physics sees, in its particulate expression, as spacetime.

Death, then, brings a dramatic reality shift in our perception; in terms of the metaphor of the reality rainbow, it is like changing the access code, so we tune in to a different frequency, chiefly the imaginal frequency. When this happens a transfiguration is wrought whereby the thinker *is* the thought, the knower *is* the known, consciousness *is* its content, without passing through the one-way world of time which requires mind to make in matter what it seeks to know in song.

These are difficult notions but they will, I hope, become clearer as we work our way through this chapter. The concept I have put forward allows us to make quite specific predictions about the way death changes the quality of consciousness but in order to test them we need 'evidence'. Until quite recently it would have seemed impossible to obtain any 'evidence' that would survive the test of rational scrutiny. But this prohibition has been lifted, in part, by the very science that once enforced it. There are many people in the modern world—quite literally millions—who have passed through the experience of dying and *returned to tell us what it was like*. Advances in medical technology have meant that many people who 'die' of cardiac arrest, for example, are 'brought back' by the controlled application of electric shock and the administration of the hormone adrenalin.

To understand what follows we must be clear on one thing. These people are not 'brain dead', otherwise their biological brains could not support their revitalised minds. But they are often 'clinically dead' in terms of the accepted medical criteria. In many cases their heartbeats have ceased, their breathing has stopped and, in some instances, even the repetitive blips their brainwaves trace on video screens have ebbed away, leaving only the monotonous flatline that is the acknowledged signature of death. But here is the remarkable thing. On recovery, about one in three of these individuals who are pronounced 'clinically dead' report a striking phenomenon called a *near-death experience* (NDE). Despite considerable differences in cultural symbolism this NDE has a 'common core' of shared experience irrespective of age, gender, educational background or type of 'death', suggesting that it is, potentially at least, a universal human experience. While there is no unanimity about what is happening, I see no reason to doubt that near-death experiencers have taken the first faltering steps along the road we may all take at the supreme crisis of life, when our time-trapped reality flickers like a fading vision on the edge of the greatest change our minds will make. Using their eyes let us look through the veil. With the logic of science as our censor let us try and make sense of the unsettling things they say.

The first element of the NDE is something our discussion of consciousness has made us familiar with. These people report a *separation* between their focus of consciousness and their bodies, so that they reach the *disembodied state* we spoke of earlier, severed from all sources of sensory input. Many NDErs say they feel as though they are floating above their bodies, watching, almost like disinterested spectators, the attempts of medical staff to revive them. One man who almost died in hospital during leukemia therapy described it like this:

> I became aware of my spirit, or whatever you want to call it,
> being up in a corner of the room and looking down on my body
> with doctors and nurses, and all the people and hospital
> paraphernalia being brought into the room and piled on my chest
> and so forth. I could not feel any of this at the time it was
> happening, but I was like a spectator looking down on this from
> up in the corner of the room. I didn't have any regrets or anything,
> it just felt kind of strange.[88]

These people are quite emphatic that they are still there, body and all, even though they can see their physical body lying on the operating table 'beneath' them. As another man put it:

> I could feel my body, and it was whole. I know that. I felt whole,
> and I felt that all of me was there, though it wasn't.[89]

What has happened? Simply said, wave-structured knowing has uncoupled from particulate mind, the dying brain has ceased to be able to collapse wave functions, consciousness has passed beyond any capacity to 'make' reality and is now liberated into the timeless reality of its own songline. Even though it is disembodied it feels bodily complete because its post-mortem knowing carries the memory of the experiences it underwent, so the knowing of its 'present' is built upon its knowing of its past, down the entire songline of its life, and this songline is structured round the sense of bodyself that was the former focus of its vision.

This first element of the NDE means that, straight away, we can test a key prediction from my hypothesis, so that we can sense whether or not the road we are following is the right

one. Let's look first at *time*. I have indicated that knowing
has a harmonic wave structure that is not subject to serial time
as we experience it in everyday life. This being so, individuals
passing through an NDE should lose all sense of the linear
time that structures awareness in the waveband of ordinary
waking reality, leaving their disembodied knowing conscious
only of the all-at-once timelessness, the 'everlasting now', that
is the hallmark of mystical insight. What do we find? Listen
to an American woman describing her 'life review'—the replay
of one's life that is another integral part of the 'core' NDE:

> I can't exactly describe it to you, but it was just all there. It was
> just all there at once, I mean, not one thing at a time, blinking on
> and off, but it was everything, everything at one time.[90]

This dissolution of the sequential time-sense is not described
in these literal terms by all NDErs but what is almost universal
is their insistence that time in the post-mortem state is, in
some impossible-to-describe way, *different* from the this-after-
that structuring of ordinary experience. The following account
from another American NDEr called Barbara captures the flavour
of what many try to say:

> And then it was like I moved through, on to where I am
> now . . . I don't want to give the idea that this was linear,
> because it wasn't linear. It was almost like that might have been
> the focal point and then things would branch out in every
> direction and I was getting different connections with different
> people.[91]

Compare this with yet another illuminating description given
by a Swedish NDEr:

> Time was not passing in the usual manner. The episodes of my life
> were not replayed like a movie. An entire episode—with its

beginning, its middle and its end—stood out as an entity; it was possible to see simultaneously every little action or spoken word with its emotion . . . tacked to it. With an adult description it was as if we were able to wander back and forth in a static landscape the features of which were not trees and hills but actions, words and emotions.[92]

Indeed, if one had to describe in experiential terms the static four-dimensional spacetime landscape that science says is real, one could hardly do better than use these words.

A second and critical prediction of my hypothesis follows from the fact that once the brain has 'died' (in clinical death) it can no longer collapse waves into 'sharp-edged' things, particles or words. So the songline that is 'you' after death must communicate with other songlines by resonance alone, melding seamlessly into the music they encode. This unimpeded communication must live out the one-to-one *communion* of wave forms that occurs when the knower *becomes* the known, the singer *becomes* the song, enacting an automatic transfer of thought, a wordless 'telepathy'.

In the light of this prediction, listen to Janis who almost died as a result of an automobile accident:

Oh, yes. In fact, I should say . . . there wasn't a transfer of words. I mean, no words were spoken. It's like thinking a thought and having them know it and answer it immediately. I mean, it's transference of thought. It was instantaneous.[93]

Or listen to Tom who almost suffocated to death in 1978:

This communication is what you might call telepathic. It's absolutely instant, absolutely clear. It wouldn't even matter if a different language was being spoken . . . whatever you thought and attempted to speak, it would be instant and absolutely clear. There would never be a doubtful statement made.[94]

103

So it all fits, it hangs together. So far we seem to be on the right track.

To go more deeply into the meaning of the NDE it is useful to turn away for a moment from the NDE as it is documented in the West and look at the older cultures of the East where dying has always been an accepted and integral part of living. The people of Tibet have evolved a remarkable death-bed ritual which is evidently based on a longstanding and convincing familiarity with the dying process. In their *Book of the Dead*, the Tibetans speak of *bardo* states which map in remarkable detail the unfolding of the NDE that Westerners have come to know. The word 'bardo' means 'gap', in the special sense of the word in which I have used it before—the silence between the sounds. Listen, for example, to what the *Book of the Dead* says to the just-dead spirit:

> Do not be afraid or bewildered. You have what is called a mental
> body of unconscious tendencies, you have no physical body of
> flesh and blood, so whatever sounds, colours and rays of light
> occur, they cannot hurt you and you cannot die . . . Know this to
> be the bardo state.[95]

This matches precisely what Westerners who have undergone an NDE say of the 'disembodied' state of their consciousness.

So let us probe further into the NDE. In its next phase many NDErs report a sensation of 'going down a tunnel'. It may be, as astronomer Carl Sagan suggests, that the tunnel represents a replay of the moment of birth, that the mind at the climactic crisis of death draws on its deepest archetypal image, that of being born.[96] It would be a rich kind of metaphor if it were true, for the instant of death is, in a symbolic sense, a moment of birth, the emancipation of spirit into the imaginal realm.

But the inner meaning of the NDE stems from what happens 'next'. Rather than pre-judge the issue, I ask you simply to listen to what real people say as they struggle to describe in words that which is untellable in any words that are.

> I just found myself in this extremely *bright light* and felt absolute peace. I feel the light and the peace were one . . . I had no sense of separate identity. I was in the light and one with it.[97]

> It's something which becomes you and you become it. I could say, 'I was peace, I was love'. I was the *brightness*. It was part of me.[98]

> It was just pure consciousness. And this enormously bright light seemed almost to cradle me. I just seemed to exist in it and be part of it . . . and the feeling just became more and more and more ecstatic and glorious and perfect'.[99]

So the core of the NDE is an encounter with *light*. But what is this light? Imagine a prism and imagine the entire visible spectrum going backwards through that prism, so that the different colours of the rainbow become the singular white light that includes and encompasses them all, so that the Many becomes the One. Is this an apt metaphor? Perhaps. But the reality is as beyond language as the experience is without precedent. Listen again to the actual words of near-death survivors. The emphasis is mine.

> As I became one with this omnipresent light, its *knowledge* became my *knowledge*. I was in a single instant what my life had been and what had been of *meaning* in my life.[100]

> You're *all-knowing*, and everything is part of you . . . it's just so beautiful. It was eternity.[101]

> The second most magnificent experience . . . is you realise that you are suddenly in communication with *absolute, total knowledge*. It's hard to describe . . . you can think of a question . . . and immediately know the answer to it.[102]

These words give us a vital clue—that the light is exactly what we would expect—*knowing*. I believe in death our knowing joins the totality of knowing so that All is One. Here, without let or hindrance, the lover is the loved, the knower is the known, the thinker is the thought. In this unconditional unity, the deep dictum of the Hindu faith is realised as experiential truth: *tat tsvam asi—thou art that*. You are whatever you think of. Within certain limits, you have only to imagine something to *be* it.

One American NDEr who went very deeply into the near-death experience describes his amazement at being able to 'alter reality' by mere effort of will:

> Then, as I studied the landscape, a lifetime interest in photography prompted me to think that the landscape I admired so greatly would be even better balanced if a certain mountain was repositioned to the other side. Immediately it moved to where I had imagined it! It was difficult at first to believe, but the experience was more real to me than anything on earth and I knew it had happened. Then, as I puzzled over this, I wondered if I could move it back, and it immediately shifted accordingly.[103]

This is not to say, however, that post-mortem consciousness is totally fluid in the sense that the individual possesses *absolute* freedom to exercise his or her volition as they please. Human imagination is actually quite limited in scope. Who, 200 years ago, could have imagined things like pulsars, microchips, supersonic flight? The difference between imaginal consciousness and physical consciousness is that the boundaries that characterise the latter do not exist in the former. In the imaginal consciousness the knowing of one can access the knowing of all and vice versa. Trained Yogis apparently can reach a lower version of this state but here, in the NDE, is the limit of the process for us so far. All knowing, seamlessly combined in One, the music that is when all the varied songlines that are blend together in the self-tuning singing of the cosmic symphony. This is the in-depth meaning of the word 'universe', whose two roots spell out uni-verse—*one song*.

This aspect of the NDE illuminates for me, a deep inner meaning in T.S. Eliot's words:

> Time past and time future
> Allow but a little consciousness.
> To be conscious is not to be in time . . .[104]

When we attempt to make verbal contact with other people in ordinary life we have to 'drop stones in the pond', creating sharp-edged things—words—to cross the gap between speaker and listener. This is a clumsy mode of interaction because it cramps communication into a serial, one-after-the-other, sequence. Similarly, our picture of the world is cramped into a time-slit, one-after-the-other, linearity because while we are only conscious of what is immediately in front of our eyes at any one moment, we have to move our field of vision incessantly in order to expand it. What this means is that there is a profound sense in which *while we are conscious in time we are not conscious at all*. But in resonant interaction there is an automatic expansion of consciousness because, by its very nature, wave communication obliterates boundaries by bringing 'thoughts' into instantaneous and unimpeded 'harmony'.

In this context, notice how exactly this 'core' part of the NDE—the experience of the light and knowing—fits the predictions of the wave theory of resonance: 'I had no sense of separate identity'; 'I was the brightness'; 'I just seemed to exist in it and be part of it'. This is not the realm of common experience. In the world of 'collapsed waves', when two particulate objects come into contact they retain their individuality: two tables which touch remain two tables. But when two waves reinforce each other, they lose their separate identity altogether, melding completely into the richer harmonic of their blended essence. Just so, the post-mortem knowing of an NDEr lacks the separating 'edges' that define our waking consciousness because his or her songline is now inextricably part of the seamless vibrational knowing in which all is one and one is all.

The act of consciousness is an act of integration, and insights are 'integrations in depth'. What happens during deep insight is that items of awareness that entered experience at different 'times' fuse into simultaneous 'music' as the wave forms that encode them 'resonate in harmony'. Thus what memory 'sees' as an unconnected, time-structured sequence, insight 'knows' as a musical 'resonance'. Expansion of consciousness at the near-death moment has just this quality of synthesis, highlighted by a dissolving of all hitherto axiomatically accepted boundaries, including the boundary around the 'self'. An Australian NDEr, Professor John Wren-Lewis, articulates this sense of unimpeded unity in these words:

> It's as if everything was there and everybody was there. The sense was of absolute, total fulfilment. And yet there was no sense that I was there. That's the most extraordinary thing—John vanished at that moment.[105]

This seems like the end of the journey, the vision we see when the faulted fractures of our time-trapped eyes die to the brightness of the light of knowing. But I have made frequent reference to the fact that the equations of the inner world have the same, almost mathematical, symmetry as those of the outer. As they must, because outer and inner are complementary aspects of the same thing. Just as there is a bright side to the message of the NDE so, in equal measure, there is a dark. This dark aspect is inescapably built into our central postulate: consciousness *is* its content. This means that your post-mortem knowing is the sum of its prior activity, the songline it has made of its experiences. The songline of your life is not a knitted thread of mere facts, of items of awareness linked together; rather, it is a faithful record of the *choices you have made. It thus bears living witness to the way you have lived your life*, whether you have lived it in the service of others or in the service of ego.

One of the few men to fully understand the implications of this is the American researcher, Kenneth Ring. He sums it up beautifully:

> We are at this very moment writing the script for our own after-
> death imaginal drama . . . we ourselves are the shapers of our
> soul's destiny . . . Not just what we are in our essence, but how
> we have in fact lived will be evident—perhaps painfully so—after
> death. For there, what was subjective becomes imaginally
> objective.[106]

The great master of mythology, Joseph Campbell, called this post-mortem crisis the 'descent to heaven'[107], to underscore a remarkable insight—that post-mortem consciousness appears to 'fall' from a justly perfect state of union with the ineffable light of collective knowing into *whatever level of imaginal consciousness is appropriate to the knowing you carry into death from life.* Thus, unless one has lived the life of a saint, most after-death states of consciousness cannot 'stay in the light', they fall into a lower level in the rainbow of consciousness.

And here the ordeal begins. From out of nowhere, or so it seems, strange images threaten the frightened soul, making real the menace implicit in T.S. Eliot's words:

> Eyes I dare not meet in dreams
> in Death's dream kingdom . . .[108]

The Western mind tends to deny or reject this; it seems like a relapse into superstition. But the Tibetan *Book of the Dead* offers us a credible explanation for this dark phase of the bardo journey. Since it goes more deeply into the experience of dying than any Western account known to us, it illuminates signposts on the road through death that few people in the West have seen. So to delve more deeply into this aspect of the mystery, to see beyond the portal into the growing mist into which the pioneering footsteps of the NDErs vanish, we must use this ancient text, perhaps the only guide we have.

At this crisis point of the death experience, the *Book of the Dead* admonishes the departed 'spirit' to understand clearly just what it is that it 'sees':

> Now when the bardo of dharmata [essence of reality] dawns upon
>   me,
> I will abandon all thoughts of fear and terror,
> *I will recognise whatever appears as my projection*
> and know it to be a vision of the bardo;
> now that I have reached this crucial point
> I will not fear the peaceful and wrathful ones,
> *my own projections.*[109]

It is easy to understand what this means. What you carry into that climactic moment of death is *what you are*—no more, no less. Once your physical senses no longer operate, you are fully and irredeemably an imaginal knowing that is the sum of all the experiences it has blended in the songline of its life. That imaginal 'self' carries into death the precise measure of the unfinished business—the anxieties, fears, envys, hates, prejudices—it had not resolved in life. In the bardo state these *inner feelings* are manifested as *outer images*. In thou-art-that awareness you see the good and bad aspects of your own nature as actual 'realities', for here your innermost hopes and terrors are made flesh and given substance by the unimpeded power of your own imagination. This is the 'Kingdom' of Jesus' words—'when the inner *is* the outer . . .'—when your soul sees itself, as in a mirror in which the explicated nightmares of your soul's pathology dance in tortured harmony with the radiant creations of your heart's goodness.

What is happening? And why? I believe the answer is simple. If you are troubled by a deep-rooted emotional illness and you go to a psychiatrist, the first thing she will do is to ask you for your case history, that is, she will invite you to tell her the story of your life so she can uncover the root of the unresolved guilt or suffering that is poisoning your psyche. In this way you become aware of the source of your suffering and in that act of recognition the 'block' which it imposed can be lifted and the healing which it prevented can commence. In much the same way, the bardo state is the redemptive laboratory of the soul's catharsis, the court where it passes judgement on itself. Just as a psychiatrist can only help you heal yourself if you *truthfully* tell your story in words, so, in the bardo state, you can only heal yourself by reliving your story in utter vulnerability and all-revealing knowing. Accordingly, a remarkable feature of the core NDE is *the replay of one's entire life history*, the panoramic life review. Listen to how one NDEr describes it:

> For me, it was a total reliving of *every* thought I had ever thought, *every* word I had ever spoken, and *every* deed I had ever done; plus the effect of each thought, word, and deed on everyone and anyone who had ever come within my environment or sphere of influence . . .[110]

Notice the hidden message of this. In the panoramic life review you do not simply 'see' your past life unroll before your eyes as in a movie; you *know* all the pain you have caused, because *you feel it yourself*. In death as in life you still are all you once were. As you 'resonate' with each reactivated wave form from your past, you become one with it and, because nothing in the 'one song' state can stand apart from anything else, *you also become one with its consequences*: if you caused suffering, you yourself suffer; if you engendered joy, you are yourself made joyful.

Thus the perfect exactitude of the moral equation: *the love you gave, you now receive; the pain you caused, you now feel.* Listen to this simple account:

> When the light appeared, the first thing he said to me was 'What do you have to show me that you've done with your life?', or something to this effect. And that's when these flashbacks started . . . the things that flashed back came in the order of my life, and they were so vivid. The scenes were just like you walked outside and saw them, completely three dimensional, and in colour. And they moved. For instance, when I saw myself breaking the toy, I could see all the movements. It wasn't like I was watching it all from my perspective at the time.[111]

This NDEr, a woman, speaks of the light as 'he'. I see no significance in that. Each individual views this 'light' through the prism of their own experience. I mention it here only so you are not distracted from the next part of her description.

> He was trying to show me something in each one of these flashbacks. It's not like he was trying to see what I had done—he knew already—but he was picking out these certain flashbacks of my life and putting them in front of me so that I would have to recall them.

> All through this, he kept stressing the importance of love . . . He pointed out to me that I should try to do things for other people, to try my best. There wasn't any accusation in any of this, though. When he came across times when I had been selfish, his attitude was only that I had been learning from them, too.

Here is the whole point of it. The life review only makes sense in relation to some yardstick of unchallengeable comparison. *That yardstick is love.* If there is one thing all NDErs agree on it is just this, that the light they see is not just light but *knowing*, and not just knowing but *love*, love made both manifest and absolute, love that seeks no reward and requests no penalty, love that simply *is*.

Another example brings out the depth of this point:

> . . . all of a sudden—quote, unquote—'my life passed before me'. But it was not my life that passed before me nor was it a three-dimensional caricature of the events in my life. What occurred was every emotion I have ever felt in my life, I felt. And my eyes were showing me the basis of how that emotion affected my life. What my life had done so far to affect other people's lives using the feeling of pure love that was surrounding me as the point of comparison. And I had done a terrible job. God! I mean it . . . Lookin' at yourself from the point of how much love you have spread to other people is devastin'. You will never get over it.[112]

Here, in the simple words of a humble man, is the core truth. The meaning of death is not what happens in the bardo state, it is what you do in *this* life—how you use the gifts you have been given, how you overcome the handicaps you inherited. And those you made.

My task up to this chapter has been to try and explain why I believe that consciousness survives death. This chapter deals with the consequences of that survival in a context where thought is no longer impeded by the limitations of matter. What emerges from this is the focused form of a simple truth that we have seen over and over again during our shared exploration. The mathematics of the inner universe are as uncompromisingly exact as those of the outer. We are 'judged' not *for* our selfishness but *by* it. And not by any external 'God' but by our harshest critic, *ourselves*.

It seems that the division between science and morality, like all boundaries, is ultimately false. So, again let us turn to what has been the theme and the foundation stone of our shared journey. What are we? Who are we? At this point we alter our whole perspective, for the revelatory lesson of this chapter is that the dreadful images that haunt us in the bardo state are *real*.

But they are not *true*.

Chapter 10

shards of truth

Our journey has brought us to the brink of an unexpected possibility, that *morality has a scientific basis*, that the link between the two key questions—'What is real?' and 'What is true?'—lies in the domain of the very values that science has so long denied.

In a sense this possibility has been inherent in almost everything we have discussed to date. Earlier we saw how one of the simplest measurable units of experience—an electron—exists as a paradoxical composite of two mutually exclusive states, wave and particle. As we dug deeply into the nature of thought we saw that this wave/particle duality explains and expresses the worlds of mind and matter that our Western tradition sees as separate. We came to see that the wave/particle duality of the electron is an apt metaphor for the complementary coupling of the inner world of subjective (wave-structured) experience and the outer world of objective (particle-structured) observation, understanding at last the special sense in which it can be said that all that lies before our eyes is fashioned behind them.

If subject and object are coupled, then it is obvious that

the world of 'facts' cannot stand apart from the invisible software of value-judgements that organises it. So it is not enough to ask of an idea, 'Is it true?'. At this stage of our journey we must also ask, 'Is it *right*?'.

On the surface, the question, 'How does one measure the rightness of an idea?' sounds too complex to pose, let alone answer. I suggest not only that there is an answer but that the answer is very simple. In my view, *rightness is to be measured—always—by the degree to which it serves the good of the whole, not the ambition of the part.* This is because the ultimate truth of the universe—across all wavebands of reality—is contained in the sacred insight, *all is one.*

This is one of those items of awareness that is so obvious we usually fail to grasp what it means. We find it easier to see distant images than things that are in front of our eyes. So let me reduce the issue to a simple question: 'How do we know what is true?' which allows me to give an equally simple answer: 'The *more* we see, the more we see *truly*'.

Suppose you focus your eyes on a pebble, excluding all else from your vision. You see the pebble (in a sense) 'truly' but you see the world (in a sense) 'falsely' because your vision is locked on to a single image. And if you think in relative terms, asking 'Which is *more* true, pebble or world?' there is only one answer and that answer is unequivocal, for *the pebble is not the world*. When you see the part at the expense of the whole you are restricting your reality, making visually small what is actually large, seeing not the One that is All but the one that is all you see.

At the level of simple seeing there is no moral judgement. This is the way our optical sight evolved. We survived the long ages of our animal ancestry by fine-tuning just this capacity to restrict our vision to the 'here' and 'now'. But we are now leaving biology and entering cognition; we are not talking about survival, we are talking about truth. So here is the missing clue, the key that unlocks the riddle. A thing that stands alone cannot, in any meaningful sense, be true, for the central fact of the universe's reality is that everything hangs together. By focusing on a pebble you may see one item of the world's fullness in significant detail, but the pebble's own 'selfness'— its ability to *be* the thing you see—depends on the rocks which support it, the kind of light that illuminates it, the direction from which that light comes, the wind and the water which shaped it and the myriad forces that, over time, will reduce it to dust. For this also is 'true', that the pebble you see at any one moment is only a snapshot of reality, a single time-frame in a movie reel.

This brings us to another issue which is absolutely central to the message of this book. To get to its essentials let us deliberately go back inside our own heads and look at the world as we are used to doing, seeing it 'out there' from the perspective of 'in here'. Then watch the shift in perception that happens when that perspective is reversed. Professor John Wren-Lewis captured the essence of this switch when he spoke of the radical way his NDE had changed the manner of his seeing:

> The feeling was one of immense depth; it's like having been to a
> place before the world was and then coming back and seeing all
> this [the world] from that space and not, as I used to, from inside
> my head.[113]

The consequences of this kind of shift in perspective are readily understood. If you tried to insult a person who had made this kind of transition completely, you would see in their eyes not the protective reflex of indignant ego—'How dare you do this to me!'—but the reflected face of understanding—'Why are you doing this to yourself?'.

This re-lensing of vision brings into sharp focus the source of the difficulty we have with perception. Because most of our sensory apparatus is located within our heads, our heads become the natural focus from which we see the world. Our heads become the focus for our sense of 'self'. But it is precisely this fixation with self that predisposes our minds to develop the sense of ego that most of us confuse with self. And *ego at its very root is untrue*, a deception our minds practise upon themselves.

Here is the very nub of the problem. *Ego is a mental construction.* And the essence of ego is *separation*. You are not just a self, you are a *separate* self. That is the legacy of the trauma of birth when 'you' came potentially into being by virtue of the act that severed you from your mother. This pivot-point, when one became two, is both your blessing and your curse, your power and your penalty. It means that your mentality from its genesis has been grounded in separation, even though the reality it samples is seamless, without boundaries, one white light that becomes a rainbow of many colours only when passed through the fracturing prism of the ordinary senses.

Self and ego are not the same. This is the most important distinction I have to make in this book. Self is an imaginal reality and it is one that, by and large, serves us well. Each of us is a valid and significant part of creation, we are sons and daughters of the stars and we have a right be here. So long as we see ourselves in this light, as co-creative partners in the collective enterprise of consciousness, we are both whole and wholesome. But ego is a corruption of that sense of self, flawed fatally by its central feature, which is to see itself as all-important, not an organic part of the world but the reason why the world exists.

Ego is the *truth inverted.* As it sees things, ego does not exist to serve the universe; rather, the universe exists to serve ego. We must never confuse self-respect, our valid sense of participating in the world for the good of all, with ego, our invalid sense of possessing the world for the good of one. The basic fallacy of ego shows through in the impossible agenda

118

it sets itself, which is to make 'true' what is not true. Ego believes itself set apart as the centre and the source, when the self that gives it being is dependent on the world for its very existence. The bread we eat has been baked by others, the oxygen we breathe is the gift of a plant, the atoms we embody are the gift of a star, the knowledge we take for granted is the freely-given legacy of a host of prior thinkers who, in the lonely labour of long hours, struggled to understand the puzzles of their time; we can only be what we are because they were what they were.

Each waveband of reality is filled with items that are different but not separate. Differences are part of the richness and colour of the world; you can look on an ant and a butterfly and say truthfully 'these two are different'. But you cannot look on them and say truthfully 'these two are separate'. When we discussed the deep reality of an atom of iron we discovered that a lineage of apparently separate objects—the star that created it, the soil which incorporated it, the red cells which use it—are all connected staging posts along the long road you yourself travelled as the cosmos grew from simplicity into sentience. Nothing stands apart from anything else. All things are interlinked. If this seamless chain of woven interconnection were severed at but a single link, the universe would become smoke and blow away.

None of this explains the all-important link between truth and rightness, so I ask you to think back to the childhood saying, 'Oh what a tangled web we weave when first we practise to deceive'. Can you remember a time when you made up a story to save yourself from punishment? Perhaps you told your parents you had finished your homework so you could watch a TV program you especially wanted to see. Once you had committed yourself to that particular lie you had to invent other 'fibs' to keep up the pretence. Until finally you gave yourself away because something you said in a different context did not fit the house of cards your lying had built. This is the inevitable outcome of lying—that sooner or later the connection breaks, the house of cards collapses. So if you ask me, 'Why are untruths wrong?' I will answer, '*Because untruths cannot build a world*'.

I can develop this concept in a way that may startle some readers. Many physicists are attracted to the 'many worlds' model of reality. In terms of this model, each choice we make creates two parallel universes, each complete with its own copy of space and time and each containing its own representation of the consciousness of the human observer.[114]

We can represent a choice by a Y node, that is, a point of decision where we have two mutually exclusive options branching in different directions. Suppose you are hesitating over whether to buy a new ski pullover. The Y node in this case is:

yes (pullover bought)   no (pullover not bought)

In the parallel universe explanation, at the point of choice the universe clones off two identical copies, alike in every respect except that in A you buy the pullover whereas in B you do not. In A, you are completely unaware of your partner cosmos which contains the choice you think you did not make, and vice versa.

In the pullover example, the choice carries no moral stigma. However, now consider a Y node where the choice is between dropping a bomb which you know will kill someone, or not dropping it and facing a court-martial. Let us attach the appropriate tags of 'right' (for the good of all) and 'wrong' (for the good of one) to these:

wrong choice   right choice
yes (bomb dropped)   no (bomb not dropped)

On the face of it, the parallel worlds interpretation makes a mockery of any system or morality because every act of choice in favour of 'right' automatically and inevitably creates its 'wrong' opposite. However, here is the point of the example. This is only true if each choice stands apart from other choices. But the whole message of this book is that this is impossible. If everything is interconnected then *each choice has to be judged in the light of all other choices because the part has no meaning outside the whole.* Acts of selfishness have the effect of weakening the links that bind universes together whereas acts of compassion and cooperation have the effect of strengthening them; thus, ultimately, a cosmos of selfish choices unravels and disintegrates. Choices, therefore, bring about a kind of cosmological Darwinism, leading us to predict that, in the final analysis, only 'unselfish' worlds survive. The significance of this is that, in this context, justice and tolerance are not human inventions but cosmological principles, the very foundations upon which worlds are built.

This speculation is consonant with the viewpoint we have built up in a progressive way throughout preceding chapters, namely that consciousness builds knowing by integrating the input of experience. This bringing together of different things, this weaving of many threads into one cloth, of many notes into one song, is always guided by the principle of *internal consistency*. Why? Because realities that are not self-consistent, that do not 'hang together', sooner or later unravel and blow away. Take mathematics for example: if a new mathematical formula is not consistent with the existing body of mathematical truth, then either the new formula is 'wrong' or the entire text is 'wrong'. They cannot both be right and be true.

Our problem as human beings is that the very way our minds operate depends on the principle of separation. To create the conceptual world our minds inhabit, we use our imaginal realities as labels, as identity, tags, *names*. So across the seamless fabric of the universe's truth we draw the symbolic lines of our imagination, to let us to find our way around. In consequence, everything is divided by the very act that names it; the world is divided into mind and matter, the human is divided into body and soul, the territorial world is divided into a host of nations, the sacred sense is divided into a host of sects. What is worse, the act of division often breeds an attitude of antagonism among the categories it creates. There is not merely a division of the world into mind *and* matter but an implication that mind is somehow set *against* matter, body *against* soul, nation *against* nation, faith *against* faith. Remember Robert Grave's words:

> Naming is treacherous
> for names divide
> truths into less truths . . .

At this transitional stage of our evolution we are trapped in this mode because language itself, by its very nature, interrupts the shared resonances of knowing, fracturing truth. While we sing the words we focus on the singing and forget about the song.

This principle of separation is partly the legacy of science's attempts to place an intentional distance between observer and observed. The idea that human beings can experiment with nature in such a way that the experimenter does not influence the outcome of the experiment lies at the core of the scientific method; it is the basis of the doctrine of objectivity. Yet the whole testimony of this text, the inner message of quantum physics, is that observer and observed, seer and sight, knower and known, are inseparably linked, resonating together in the shared song of knowing.

Part of our difficulty is that today's culture confuses knowing, which is born of *insight*, with memory, which is born of *repetition*. Insight comes in its own time, when the mind is ready, and it transfigures information into wisdom, whereas recollection is a mental property that enables people merely to access experience without, in any meaningful way, understanding it. Which explains the great spiritual impoverishment of our age. For knowing, deep knowing, is a prize that can be won only by voyaging, as we have done together, into the deeps of consciousness and paying in full the price of pain and patience that is demanded of those who passionately need to know.

Why does ego go through this endless process of boundary-making? Because the consciousness that lights it knows that its boundaries are untrue. So what does ego do to suppress the lie it is? Yes, like any liar that is caught out, ego denies the charge, seeking strenuously for ways to justify the crime it has committed upon the inner truth of the soul's reality. How? By bringing into itself everything that is other. Why? Because if it can trap 'otherness' inside its own 'self' it can reassure itself that the lie it has told is, in fact, no lie—that the fiction on which it is founded is not false. From this unavoidable *insecurity of ego* spring all the needs, desires, envies, hatreds, jealousies that torment the soul. From this insecurity of ego comes the need of all religious fanatics to convert others, that is, to remove the threat their otherness poses to a collective ego's sense of corporate religious identity by bringing all the differing interpretations within the familiar ambit of its own self-image. From the basic insecurity of ego springs the desire of nations to conquer others, to raise over the ruins of one nation's defeated otherness the symbolic flag of another nation's triumphant 'self'.

For this is also the nature of ego: because it is a fiction, it is driven insatiably to 'prove its point', to affirm the reality it does not have. Thus it ever seeks not merely to 'stay where it is' (for that would mean, in time, looking at what it is) but to extend its boundaries as if, by making the size of the lie bigger, it can somehow make the guilt of its trespass less. So egos—individual and corporate—are always, by their very nature, driven to *expand*. What else is a war of conquest but an attempt to extend the boundary round the collective self?

Ego is forever insecure. All fabrications are insecure because they are *untrue*. Unable to face the fact of its own falsehood, ego *projects* on to others those shadow-sides of self it does not want to recognise. These projections lead people to fear and persecute in others precisely those things that they fear and deny in themselves. This phenomenon of projection defines the way ego *inverts reality*, externalising its own failures, making the outer universe the simple reflection of its own fiction.

This is a central message of this book: *in the mirror of the world, ego sees only itself. Which is why it does not see at all. This is its fundamental and its fatal flaw.*

Why, then, is ego so strong, so tenacious? Because its key hook is the feeling of *centre* that makes this fiction seem the focus of the world. So rather than confront the inner lie, people will attack its outer projections; quite literally they will seek to change the world rather than change themselves. Thus it is easier for most males to degrade and assault homosexual men than to acknowledge—and accept—the feminine side of themselves; thus it was easier for Adolf Hitler to attempt to destroy the entire Jewish race than to confront—and heal— the trauma in his young manhood that made Jews the outer scapegoats for his inner self-contempt.

This is the inner meaning of the 'life review' in the bardo state. The terrors you see are projections of ego. These projections are false because ego is false. The only reality they have is the reality you give them and the strength of this reality depends absolutely on the degree to which you have made your ego the centre of your life. If you have lived for the most part self(ego)-*less*-ly, the songline of your life will be true, so you will know the projections of ego for the deceptions they are. If you have lived for the most part self(ego)-*ish*-ly, the songline of your life will be false, so you will see the bardo terrors as real and you will be trapped in an imaginal nightmare of your own making. Thus do you judge yourself. What you *are* judges what you *see*, and what you see *is* what you *are*; hence the inner meaning of the old paradox, *you have to know what you see to see what you know*.

Think in terms of the musical metaphor that is the leitmotif of this text. If the songline of your life is out of tune with the chorus of creation, it cannot become part of the uni-verse, the one song, the music that makes the world. This is why the wave form of knowing is critical to the issue of survival. It is only when wave patterns are intrinsically harmonic that they can stabilise into standing waves—waves which last. In terms of this metaphor, ego is a kind of 'static', discordant and disruptive, for a songline that is true is ever a songline that is beautiful, since beauty is truth and truth is beauty, always and without exception.

While this may sound like something which is poetically true, not factually true, the link is undeniably there. The Greek mathematician Pythagoras showed that the pitch of a musical note depends on the frequency of its vibration (see Figure 7). If a node is moved halfway along a vibrating string playing its ground note, the string plays a note an octave higher and so on. The fascinating feature of this discovery was the realisation that the chords which sound pleasing to the human ear correspond to exact divisions of the vibrating string by whole numbers. Only these whole numbers can set up standing waves; any unwhole numbers merely set up discordances and noise, by its very nature, cannot make a melody.

This is the meaning of the bardo crisis, when your inner flaws appear as your outer nightmares. What is happening during this process of self-appraisal is that your songline is struggling to free itself of the discordances that corrupt its singing. If you can purify your knowing from the noise of ego, the 'you that is truly you' can join the symphony of creation and the song you have become can meld seamlessly into the music that is. In this sense, and in this sense only, can 'you' win the immortality the ancient faiths have promised.

If the noise of ego is too strong, what happens then? Simply

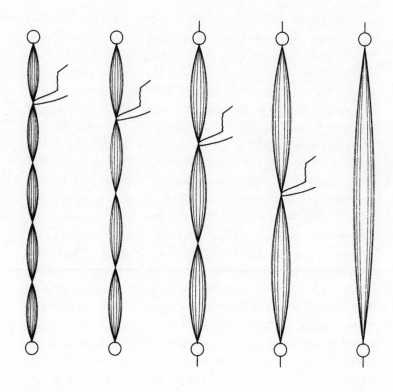

Figure 7 The pitch of a vibrating string depends on the frequency of its vibration.

put, your faulted songline disintegrates into the background static of absolute randomness, for it is a fundamental characteristic of wave mechanics that only harmonic waves can become standing waves and only standing waves can resonate together to make the song that makes the world one. So the fate of ego is not to suffer everlasting torment as the ancient faiths, in their misbegotten bigotry, believed; it is *to cease to be*, to return to the mindless jabbering of chaos that is the signature of chance. If the 'many worlds' theory is true, then this is also the fate of universes in which consciousness does not resonate harmonically with the visions it creates.

A friend of mine captured the essence of this message with a computer analogy. 'Computers,' he said, 'are like religion; both have that blessed word "save"'. Thus an author who has spent years creating and refining the book that is his life's work does not save the hundreds of trial runs he processed along the way; he saves only the finished product because this is the version that best expresses his message. He saves the version *worthy* to be saved. In just this fashion, the collective singing of the universe preserves those songlines that best harmonise with its basic themes of love and unity, abandoning without judgement those that fail to rhyme. Hence the point of my conviction that the universe is *an evolving work of art.*

I can now tie more threads of my argument together. Throughout this book I have pointed to paradox as the key to knowing on a deep level. Every great spiritual tradition has at its centre the deeply paradoxical insight, given in the Introduction: *He who loses his life shall find it.*

This is the message of the death and rebirth metaphor that pervades all religions, from the story of Osiris in Egypt to the story of Jesus in Israel. What does it mean? Simply this, that to find the true light of everlasting life, all that is false in one's being has to die. In a primitive sense, one automatically thinks of physical death, the death of the body. Jesus dies on the cross. But what is really meant is the *death of ego*, for ego is the source of falsehood. This is why all sacred traditions speak of *dying before death* as the only road to enlightenment, to the knowing of God.

When we began our journey we saw the world 'out there' from a focus 'in here'. As we progressed through the various layers of meaning of quantum physics we came to see that inner and outer, subject and object, are linked inseparably by the very act of consciousness that lets us know them. So we began to understand that the mathematics of the inner world are as unrelentingly precise and as faultlessly symmetric as those of the outer. Morality mirrors physics because morality is the subjective face of physics. So the insight 'as you give, so you receive' means that, in the equations of human interactions, giving is linked to receiving with the same inflexible exactitude as, in the equations of physics, cause is linked to effect. This 'rule' is the guideline for your life, the way you *make* in life the songline you will *be* in death, the way the universe tunes the experimental singing of its collective song.

This moral equivalence lies like a glowing jewel at the kernel of each of the world's great faiths.[115] The wise ones of Christianity said it like this:

All things whatsoever ye would that men should do to you, do ye even so unto them; for this is the Law of the Prophets (Matthew 7:12).

Those of Judaism like this:

What is hateful to you, do not to your fellow man. That is the entire law; all the rest is commentary (Talmud, Shabbat, 31a).

Those of Hinduism like this:

This is the sum of duty; do naught unto others which would cause pain if done to you (Mahabharata 5, 1517).

Those of Buddhism like this:

Hurt not others in ways that you yourself find hurtful (Udana-Varga 5, 18).

Those of Confucianism like this:

Surely it is the maxim of loving kindness; do not unto others that
you would not have them do unto you (Analects 15, 23).

Those of Taoism like this:

Regard your neighbour's gain as your own gain and your
neighbour's loss as your own loss (T'ai Shang Kan Ying P'ien).

Those of Islam like this:

Not one of you is a believer until he desires for his brother that
which he desires for himself (Sunnah).

I can round this off with a personal example. When I was
young I had an uncle who kept on his kitchen wall a framed
poem which went like this:

So many ways, so many creeds,
so many paths that wind and wind
when just the art of being kind
is all this old world needs.

This is a homespun way of expressing the golden rule. As we
have moved through the development of this book we have
seen with increasing clarity the inescapable relationship between
moral action and reaction; we have come to know that where
there is guilt there is always retribution, if not in life then
in death, for cause is tied to effect in a loop that always closes.
Bad intentions are like boomerangs—they always return to the
hand that throws them. If we live only for ourselves we may
become rich in possessions but we will be poor in relationships,
so that when, in sickness or old age, we need our friends, they
will not be there. To have a friend you must be one.

The message of this chapter is the death of ego and the
birth of truth. I will close with words from two people who

have been into that dark nimbus and seen the radiance it contains. Let me repeat the already-quoted words of John Wren-Lewis as he describes that near-death moment:

> It's as if everything was there and everybody was there. The sense was of absolute, total fulfilment. And yet *there was no sense that I was there.* That's the most extraordinary thing—John vanished at that moment.

And the result of that death of ego? In the words of a woman who 'died' during childbirth:

> I felt as though I was *awake for the first time* in my life.[116]

Or, in the more eloquently articulated words of Walt Whitman:

> I cannot be awake, for nothing looks to me as it did before or else *I am awake for the first time* and all before has been a mean sleep.[117]

This sense of awakening into fulfilled cognition highlights the depth of meaning in T.S. Eliot's insight: *to be conscious is not to be in time.*

the cosmic balance

The end of our journey is now in sight. Two things remain to be said but, as always, they are not separate, they are twin sides of a common coin.

Let us go back in imagination one last time, to that inconceivable moment when the world began, the Big Bang. One thing we can say about that just-born cosmos is that it was perfectly symmetric; matter and radiation were not divided, the forces of nature had not separated out. For a fleeting instant there was a moment of total purity, of utter and absolute simplicity. In the spirit of parable in which this text is cast we can say of this moment, All was One.

Now jump forward to a time when the cosmos is perhaps 200 million years old. The deeps of that cosmic night are unlit by stars. The universe is cold, seemingly empty, void of light and apparently barren of purpose. And then a miracle occurs as everywhere, everywhere, wonderfully, majestically, the galaxies flutter into being like snowflakes, summoned into magical existence by the exacting fulfilment of a unique set of cosmic conditions that never were before and never shall be again.[118]

What was the power that drew those congealing clouds of gas together? Overwhelmingly it was gravity, using the almost-spent ripples of the Big Bang's aftershock as 'seed crystals' around which the condensing cities of gas could grow. So, in the language of metaphor let us say of gravity what a storyteller might say, what I have already said, that it is the yearning of divided matter to again be one—the desire of fragmented energy to restore the union that was violated by the act of its birth.

Any act of creation is an act of separation. You were born when you separated from your mother's womb. In the Bible, God created the world by separating earth and sky:

> . . . and God divided the light from the darkness . . .
> And God said, Let there be a firmament in the midst of the
> waters, and let it divide the waters from the waters.

This description of creation seems puzzling when set in the context of my treatment of ego since the negative connotations that cluster round the concept of the separateness of self seem to taint any link between 'creation' and 'separation'.

We reach here a deep issue which is as alien to the Western tradition as it is integral to the Eastern. Take the simple example of a curved arc:

CONCAVE) CONVEX

In terms of the usual scientific mindset one could describe this by saying that the curved line *separates* concave from convex. But this is a shallow way of seeing for, as transpersonal writer Ken Wilber points out, the line which creates the one also automatically and inevitably creates the other.[119] The two opposites, like all opposites, are not just indissolubly linked, *each only exists by virtue of its partner.* Think back to the parable of the stone dropped into the pond. Whenever you speak, in a metaphorical sense you set up a wave by dropping

132

a stone in the water. You cannot make the wave without dropping the stone, for creation and destruction, too, are coupled—as all opposites are.

This principle focuses our attention on a dark issue few of us want to look at. The German poet Goethe wrote a play called *Faust*, based on a medieval story about a man who sold his soul to the Devil in return for all knowledge and all power. The original Faust was the perfect embodiment of ego, craving, as ego does, not sufficient power to live but absolute power to conquer, to rule, to enslave. In Goethe's version there is a crucial scene in which Faust is in his study, reading, when he is disturbed by the Devil disguised as a wandering scholar. Faust looks up and asks of the Devil, 'Who art thou?' to which the Devil offers the paradoxical reply, 'I am part of that spirit which *always wills evil and always creates good*' (my emphasis).[120] What this means is that there is a particular sense in which 'good' is only created by the 'evil' it seeks to overcome; for it is precisely *because* of pain, unrelentingly *because* of suffering, that human beings are driven to outgrow the littlenesses of their own limitations, to 'rise above themselves', to climb the mountain to see the vision.

In the West there has been an enormous reluctance to acknowledge the price that evolution asks of us for any act of transcendence. Because of this blinkered view we have tended to see either the positive side of the equation or the negative, while refusing to acknowledge the coupling between them. Thus we see trauma only in the mechanical sense of damage to be repaired, we speak of emotional illness only in the symbolism of pathology and we speak of death only in the language of denial. What we all too often overlook is the dark invitation that a crisis like illness offers us. For it is often only when our physical safety is threatened, our emotional foundations shattered and our comfort zone breached that we are challenged to change in a meaningful way, to forsake the safety of the inn for the hardship of the road, to push ourselves to the limits of our being and then to go beyond that. The invitation thus offered by crisis is almost mathematically exact, for the depth to which we can sink can also be the precise measure of the height to which we can rise.

What is true of individuals is also true of our collective humanity. To make the planet whole it first had to become sick. Very sick. Which is why the planetary crisis we see all round us is the symptom not of the world's end but of its rebirth, the visible testament to the unchanging truth that darkness begets light in just such a fashion that the one is the exact measure of the other. A young visionary, Andrew Harvey, captured the nub of this truth in powerful words. His teacher says to him:

> Now I will show you the twentieth century. Gaze with all your courage into its darkness.

> I saw writhing bodies, burning, flayed, spattered with blood. I saw bombs flowering, the faces of mad dictators as they cut open the eyes of living children, torturers masturbating over the women they had just electrocuted. I saw all these nightmares arising out of the darkness and returning to it. Then, just as I thought I would faint because I could not bear the sight and smell of so much horror, I realized, with a clarity and certainty beyond my power to express, that this terrible, unparalleled filth and depravity, this unspeakable desolation spread out over every continent and enacted in every culture, was feeding the New Light. The spiral of light rises out of the darkness.[121]

So my own conviction is that transcendence cannot be uncoupled from the suffering that makes it possible. We see here the universality of the principle of complementarity that is the essence of paradox.

Let us now turn from the symmetrically opposed elements of suffering and transcendence to those of creation and destruction with which we began this chapter. Creation and destruction are intimately tied to separation and union. In the language of the metaphor, it is the divisive Devil which separates; the function of the knowing God is to unite, for the act of knowing is the act of integration.

Synchronistically one can note here that the word religion comes from two Latin roots *re* and *ligare*—re-ligare (to bind together)—so a root meaning of religion is *that which binds together*. An act of separation divides in two what previously was one, while an act of union joins in one what previously were two. This is why an act of union is, ironically, an act of destruction, for the prior selfhood of the thing to be joined is always lost in the act that joins it. And here is exactly where the *evolving point*, the cutting edge of the cursor, is to be found. For something is often gained—the new union of separately evolved, hence different, parts may make a richer whole, a deeper depth, a more spellbinding story.

The development of science exemplifies the way this complementary dualism works, separating on the one hand and uniting on the other. The methodology of science has been to cut up, to divide, to specialise, to separate subject from object, experiment from experimenter. But the motivational thrust of science has been in precisely the opposite direction. Its passion has been to join the facts it discovers into theories, to bind them together, thus making science the companion and the heir to religion in ways neither side has suspected or understood. There were once believed to be five separate forces of Nature then, in 1887, James Clerk Maxwell discovered equations that revealed electricity and magnetism to be different aspects of the one field (electromagnetism). In the late 1960s Abdus Salam and Steven Weinberg extended this principle to encompass the weak nuclear force and electromagnetism, giving us the 'electroweak field'. Today, in the vision of contemporary physics, all forces are coming to be seen as variants of one superforce.[122] And all the while science strives to achieve its grandest triumph—the unification of all its laws into one all-encompassing *Theory of Everything*. Whether this is possible is less important at this juncture than the fact that science wants it to be possible.

So the grand design begins to emerge. The universe is rooted in paradox; it is built on two opposing processes which work together; one process *creates* by separating out the hidden richness of nature, the other *unites* the divisions that are so created, integrating the thoughts that swarm on each frequency of the reality rainbow, keeping the process in perfect pace, lest the harmony be disturbed and the singing cease and the songlines sunder.

On a cosmic scale, the creative process is what we call evolution, the progressive unfolding of the encrypted symmetries, the ongoing making of differences, the risky division of One into Many. But in parallel with this process and coupled to it has gone on its opposite, a complementary dynamic whose theme is joining, binding, uniting. Stars only shine because two atoms of hydrogen combine to make one of helium; minds only fire when unconnected facts meld into the harmonic music of an unexpected insight, for the fundamental act of knowing is an act of integration. Always.

So we have the cosmic balance, the One becomes the Many and the Many become the One. This is the dance of Shiva, the creative tension of enraptured opposites, the source of the music the world sings. As T.S. Eliot put it (my emphasis):

> At the still point of the turning world. Neither flesh nor fleshless;
> Neither from nor towards; *at the still point, there the dance is*
> But neither arrest nor movement and do not call it fixity,
> Where past and future are gathered. Neither movement from nor
>   towards,
> Neither ascent nor decline. Except for the point, the still point
> There would be no dance and *there is only the dance*.[123]

Throughout this book the still point of balance (symmetry) has occupied centre stage. A paradox is a balance which is broken. A creative act comes from the use of unbalanced power. In the Creation the balance was broken and preserved. We can now see how it all ties together, for the point of a paradox is that it reconciles opposites to make a truth. As I said in the opening chapter, opposites are not enemies but partners, linked together in a union too strong to sever; concave cannot exist without convex, up without down, light without darkness.

Any creative act, any mutation, breaks the balance of the existing world. In accordance with the law of action and reaction, that broken balance is at once restored at the higher level that results from the integration of the newly created difference. This is the paradox on which the cosmos rests, that the whole must ceaselessly break to reveal the newborn parts and the differentiated parts must ceaselessly meld to remake the enriched whole.

I can now uncover another layer of meaning in this. In Chapter 1 I stressed the significance of the recurrent use of images of darkness and water in creation myths. I believe this is because these genesis myths encode dim memories of that dark watery time in the womb, they are the imaginal children of those first unremembered memories.[124] There is a link between the deeply imprinted experience of the time in the womb and the imaginal form of the creation myth. Now each primal culture, each tribal society, thought its own creation myth was *the* creation myth, as all isolated cultures do. It was only after all myths had all been gathered together that later scholars began to see their underlying sameness. That subsequent knowing had two key features: universality—all the different myths were seen to stem from one root—and depth—the insight of unity was made the richer by the different branches on the tree, by the spectrum of colours in the imaginal rainbow of explanation. So that deep knowing closed the loop:

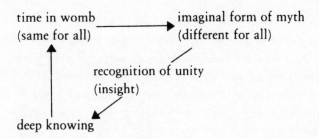

The human mind returned to its point of origin and knew it for the first time. The One gave birth to the Many and the Many returned to the One. But that One of the end was not the One of the beginning; it was significantly richer because it drew together into itself all the differences that had emerged during the process of human cultural evolution, making a textured coat of many colours, playing a symphony where once there had been only a melody. This helps us understand why T.S. Eliot's lines resonate so strongly with us, why we sense their truth without being able to explain why.

> We shall not cease from exploration
> and the end of all our exploring
> will be to arrive where we started
> and know the place for the first time.

This is only scratching the surface of the resonance, however. What is so striking is that the same metaphor works for the universe. Evolution has been going on for 15 billion years. From the Big Bang came matter and from matter came life and from life came mind. And from mind came myth. And image. And idea. Multiplying and diversifying like the living process it was. This was the *evolution of differences*. But mind, like matter, was ever obedient to the hunger that drives all desire—the urge to be One. So in tandem with the making of differences came the binding of differences. Thus here again, on the grandest possible scale, we have the same principle; the One becomes the Many and the Many become the One. *But the One of the End is not the One of the Beginning; it is richer by far because it draws together into one song all the varied notes of the chorus of creation.*

So when, during the course of this evolution, does the product of the process look back upon its own origins and know them for the first time? The answer can only be: when the universe produces conscious beings who can correctly answer the oldest of all human questions, 'Where did I come from?'. And here is the point and the purpose of it all; *we are those beings.*

That moment of critical recognition occurred during the lifetimes of most of us. Its seeds were planted when the physicist Paul Dirac noticed that the rules which govern the structure of the universe contain some strange regularities, some hidden symmetries.[125] For example, the ratio of the electromagnetic force to gravity is 10^{40} This is a huge number—10 followed by 40 zeros. The number of particles in the cosmos is 10^{80} or $10(^{40})^2$. And the age of the cosmos is 10^{40}. (We do not measure this in years for a year is simply the time it takes the earth to go round the sun. We use one of Nature's own clocks—the time it takes for light to cross the diameter of a classical electron. Since electrons are everywhere the same, this time will be universally true.)

Now these regularities are strange indeed. It is odd enough that the ratio of two of the basic forces that govern physical reality should have exactly half the value of the total mass of the cosmos. But it is even stranger that we should find the same root value for the age of the cosmos. Why? Because, unlike force and mass, time is not constant; it changes day by day, millenium by millenium.

As they pondered this point, many physicist came to a strange, awesome realisation. This time—t—could not have been other than 10^{40}. Suppose t had been 10^{37} time units, that is, in the past. At this stage in evolution we were still in the fireball.

Galaxies, stars and thinking creatures could not exist. And if t were 10^{42} time units, that is, in the future, a living earth would no longer exist; it would have been sterilised into a lump of rock by the swollen red giant our sun will become.[126] So only this 'moment' was right for us, or something like us, to evolve. It takes 10^{40} units of time for the universe to create complex creatures with brains powerful enough to surge through the limitations of matter. As the Jesuit scientist Teilhard de Chardin said:

> We already knew that everywhere the active lines of life grow warm with consciousness towards the summit. But in one well-marked region at the heart of the mammals, where the most powerful brains ever made by nature are to be found, they become red hot. And right in the heart of that glow burns a point of incandescence.

> We must not lose sight of that line, crimsoned by the dawn. After thousands of years rising below the horizon, a flame bursts forth at a strictly localised point.

> Thought is born.[127]

When Dirac saw the significance of these numbers he was not making a merely human discovery. In Dirac the universe itself saw itself for the first time, awoke in self-awareness, knew its origins and began faintly, faintly, to understand its destiny. To put this another way, when he saw the significance of the 'code-breaking' number 10^{40}, Dirac was glimpsing a hitherto unsuspected truth—that *the laws that structure the cosmos make inevitable the emergence of a mind that can know them.*[128] That moment of recognition was a truly magic moment in time for at that instant the cosmos awoke in consciousness, the songline of the universe closed back upon itself, and its circumference rang with the keyed-up resonance of a partly finished song.

But here we sense a problem that carries the burden of the sceptic's doubting. The unspoken implication of this insight is that human minds *created* the cosmos. Yet the solution to this difficulty is inherent in my words—'a partly finished song', not a finished song. At this stage of their evolution human minds can create imaginal realities, imaginal thoughts, but they cannot create physical thoughts, except at the margins of reality, where imaginal 'singings' become physical 'things'. These transfers of knowing from imaginal songlines to physical things are rare at this human moment in the cosmic story.[129] They only 'come alive' at the uncertain borderline between magic and science and they are made flimsy and illusionary by the divisions which separate the many imaginal 'dreamings' of the human species. They have no coherent reality because there is no consensus as to the 'final form' their knowing should take. *So whose mind was it that dreamed the cosmos into being?*

To answer this, let us go back to the evolutionary sequence as we came to understand it in the opening chapter:

Big Bang—hydrogen gas—proto galaxies—first generation stars—supernovae—second generation stars and planets—life—consciousness.

Let me repeat the words I used at that point. From hydrogen, the simplest of all the atoms, have come symphony orchestras, diamonds, the glimmer of dew on spiderwebs at dawn, the underwater flight of dolphins, the colours inside abalone shells, Voyager spacecraft, fractal images on computer screens, and the laser light of cognitive awareness. This is not a mechanical progression from simplicity to complexity; it is a creative act of stupendous proportions. We are the products of this evolutionary process. We are also its heirs and its trustees.

So here is the inevitable question: *Is the process over, will it stop with us?* Clearly the answer is no. We are only one chord in the songline of the universe and the cosmos does not culminate in this moment that is special to us only because we happen to inhabit it. The cosmos is *unfinished business*, a song still only partly sung, a story only half told. Beyond this human moment in the cosmic drama I see the arc of consciousness continuing to rise, the light of mind continuing to brighten, until it reaches a more critical 'magic moment', which occurs when the completed mind of the universe is able to map in melodic metaphor the process that gave rise to itself. That completed mind can think the thoughts that are the stuff of physical reality because their tuneful integration is the knowing, the consummate knowing, that structures them. At that moment of absolute climax, past and future combine in an instant of total understanding and the cosmos seals itself into the loop of becoming it has always been.

Thus it is that all realities sleep in a kind of quantum dreaming until they are awakened by the fire that comes from *recognition*, when a wave resonates between familiar images, when the child of a knowing looks back at its parent and sees it, recognises it, becomes it, for in that act of recognition the song it sings is lifted several octaves higher in the scale of creation. Then an energy that at its limit may have the searing brightness of ten trillion suns may be focused and in that intelligent act of perfected knowing a universe may be born.

Thus *was* the universe born, I believe, when the mind that was its fulfilment looked back on its origins and knew them for the first time. So that the One of the climax drew into itself the music of the Many that its beginning had set in motion, giving the end the depth the beginning lacked, for that depth comes from time, as we can now start to understand. Undergirding the whole process is the wave/particle paradox that defines reality. Only the particulate 'hardware' of mind can create the wave 'software' of thoughts and only the wave 'software' of thoughts can make the particulate 'hardware' of mind.

A simple crystal of insight tells us how the world is built: *Knowing unites in eternity what matter creates in time.*

Chapter 12

a beauty too
terrible to see

The last two chapters drew attention to a root meaning of
the word 'religion' (re-ligare) as that which binds together.
Religious myths are, in my view, humanity's first great attempt
to bind together the confusing input of experience, to make
sense of the world. Science is a child of the same impulse,
the only difference being that it does it more precisely, in a
way that makes its stories testable and its storytellers
accountable. But the bond between science and religion is very
strong, for the simple truth is this: humanity needs its story.
To give meaning to our lives, to give fire to our thoughts,
to give motive to our intentions, we need—compellingly,
achingly, almost desperately—to believe in something. That
something is always a story, a myth, a Dreaming, a theory,
something which weaves the separate threads into a common
cloth, which takes of the Many and makes it One.

I now want to 'bind together' all the many threads this
text has woven. Central to my message has been my belief
that the fundamental act of consciousness is an act of integration.
Let us re-focus our minds on what this means. We think of
consciousness in terms of the picture we paint of what we

see around us. We take this image of consciousness so much for granted that we overlook the computational feat our brains perform to create it. We assume that what we see around us is simply 'there'. But is it? If someone blind from birth suddenly recovered their sight in your presence at this moment, would they see what you see? No, they would not. They would see an amorphous fuzz, a whiteness. Like each of us, they would have to learn to see by creating the software that allows the brain to define detail and judge distance and so on. It is this learned software in our minds that enables us to construct a coherent picture of the world around us in order to make us conscious of it.

Allow me to recap and reinforce the lesson of Chapter 9. Consciousness builds its model of the world by integrating the input of experience to create knowing. Up to this point I have described this integrative capacity of consciousness only in what I can very loosely call 'left brain language', in terms of the 'head'. But it holds equally for matters of the heart. We can see the urge to integration conspicuously in the mystery we call love which, by definition, requires two sovereign individuals to abandon the selfhood of each to achieve the union of both. Note how love poetry works most powerfully when it goes beyond the individuals concerned to draw in other things, to integrate more fully, to expand that sense of oneness:

When your hand touches mine, it is the earth
that takes me—the deep grass,
and rocks and rivers; the green graves
and children still unborn, and ancestors
in love passed down from hand to hand from God.
Your love comes from the creation of the world
from those paternal fingers, streaming through the clouds that
break with light the surface of the sea.

Here, where I trace your body with my hand
love's presence has no end;
for these, your arms that hold me, are the world's.
In us, the continents, clouds and oceans meet
our arbitrary selves, extensive with the night,
lost, in the heart's worship, and the body's sleep.[130]

In this penultimate chapter we now make a crucial switch—
we ask not what consciousness is but what it may become.
How might consciousness evolve? Look at Figure 8. This shows
a two-dimensional universe called Flatland built only of the
dimensions of width and breadth.[131] This flat world is intersected
by a tubular semi-circle, which possesses the added dimension
of height. Now try and put yourself in the mental position
of an intelligent inhabitant of Flatland trying to comprehend
the reality of the three-dimensional tube. What does he see?
Two separate circles, apparently quite unconnected. However,
he notices that whenever he disturbs A he causes a corresponding
disturbance in B and vice versa; hence he deduces that a 'force'
is acting to *link* A and B.

From our more privileged three-dimensional perspective we
can see that the Flatlander's 'force' is the simple consequence
of the fact that A and B are part of the same structure. The
principle which emerges is fundamental. Things which seem
separate on one level of seeing emerge as undivided parts of
the one reality when viewed from higher levels of seeing. Or
to put it in more challenging terms: as our software improves,
the more we see as *one* things we hitherto thought were *separate*.

This, I submit, is the defining feature of the evolution of
consciousness: the increasing ability to see the interconnectedness
of things, to see the 'one' in the 'many'. The holism of a
person's consciousness is thus a litmus test of the quality of
their software or the depth of their knowing, or to put it more
provocatively, it is a measure of the *truth* of their reality.

The core message of this chapter is this: *consciousness evolves in a direction defined by ever-increasing integration.* At its limit this process becomes all-encompassing, leading to the insight that *All is One.* Which is exactly the message of the sacred traditions of the world's great faiths. We live, I believe, at a pivot-point in evolution because the two great traditions of the human species are now converging on the same spot. On the one hand we have science which, simplistically speaking, uses 'left-brain' reasoning to arrive at the conclusion that to explain anything you have to explain everything. And on the

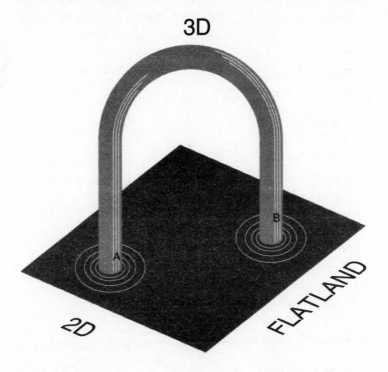

Figure 8 The two-dimensional surface of a plane (Flatland) is intersected by the twin ends of a U-tube, which has the extra dimension of height. How would an intelligent inhabitant of Flatland interpret these two seemingly separate 'circles', given that any disturbance to A always produces a corresponding effect on B?

other hand we have the sacred tradition which, simplistically speaking, uses 'right-brain' intuition to arrive at the conclusion that the part has no meaning outside the whole.

The ancient Indian text, the *Rig Veda*, captured this insight in a kind of koan:

> The letter N is made up of three lines.
> Does this mean it is more than one?[132]

Each line that enters the construction of the letter N is pointless without its companions. The meaning of each line emerges only in the combination made. This is a universal law. For all created things, our meaning is in our togetherness.

Another Indian sacred text, the *Upanishads*, expresses the same insight in these words:

> The Lord of all,
> the knower of all,
> the beginning and end of all—
> that Self dwells in every human heart.
> Look out—it's gone.
> Look in—it's gone.
> Don't look—it's gone.
> it cannot be remembered,
> it cannot be forgotten,
> It cannot be grasped by any possible means.
> It is beyond all limits and bounds.
> It is the pure oneness
> where nothing else can exist.
>
> To know it, you must become it![133]

Compare it with the core message of the scientist, David Darling:

> Even now, at the close of the twentieth century, we sense it. You and I are the infant cosmos, still only dimly aware, still only

148

conscious of things around the reality generators that are our minds. We perceive only dully, over a narrow range of wavelengths of light and sound, and we comprehend structure over only a narrow range in space and time. But, eventually, we will see X-rays and gamma rays, radio waves and gravitational waves. *And* subatomic particles. *And* whole galaxies in their most intimate detail. We shall see and understand all there is to know. What we are today will evolve to become a single universe-wide mind, so that every particle within space will be in this cosmic consciousness - free, but aware. Every particle of which you - I are made will be ultimately reconstituted in this universal mind, along with everything else. Given such a prospect, we need hardly fear our own personal deaths. For nothing ever dies. And in Deep Time we shall be as One.[134]

The theme of integration has not only been a linking theme of this book, it has provided the 'vector' which points the way to this moment we have now reached, the point of climax. Let us slow down our intake of ideas to accommodate what follows.

The act of consciousness is an act of integration and the integration of thoughts is knowing. Let me reword this slightly and say: *The act of consciousness is an act of union*. The point of this chapter and the message of this book become clear when I now say: *The act of union is an act of love*.

In Chapter 1 I developed an allegory that allowed us to speak of the force of gravity as *desire*. Even then it was obvious that this allegory encompassed the other forces that collectively make the world. Indeed science increasingly sees these different forces as varied faces of the one 'superforce'. So all the seemingly separate forces of Nature—electromagnetism, the weak and strong nuclear forces and gravity—individually and collectively express the desire of divided matter to restore the union that was violated by the act of its birth. In the same spirit of parable we can say that each act that quenches those yearnings in union is an act of *love*. When two atoms of hydrogen meld into one of helium there is a brightening of love. It is a coarse and ignorant form of love because it affects chiefly the physical waveband of consciousness, but it is love nonetheless. When a man and a woman mate, there is a brightening of love. This is a hybrid form of love, expressed partly on a complex level of physical consciousness as sex and partly on a psycho-spiritual level as the loss of selfhood. When two ideas join in the act of insight there is a brilliant *flash* of love which, in the case of an integration-in-depth, is like a supernova of the mind. This is an intelligent form of love because it illuminates the imaginal waveband.

Each of these acts of love is an integration. Which means it is an act of consciousness, an advance in knowing. Each act extinguishes desire in union. Each act reduces the pervading loneliness of the divisions that remain. A fraction. *And each act brightens the light of the universe.* A fraction. This brightening is literal in the case of the union of hydrogen into helium (it is what produces starlight[135]) but it is no less real in the case of insight. Indeed, we use an image of light when we speak of insight as a *flash* of inspiration. And this is why the broadening of consciousness is aptly called en*light*enment.

Our tendency to see the love that emerges from the melding of hydrogen as unrelated to and different from the love that emerges from the melding of man and woman is a hangover from our tendency to see connected things as separate. The love that makes starlight seems a more awesome form of love than the love that makes children because stars are big and children are small. But to think this way is to confuse the relative importance of quantity and quality. How big is an idea?

However, while the love that makes starlight is not separate from the love that makes children, the integration that produces it is much lower on the scale of consciousness. Among other things, stars shine because two identical atoms of hydrogen merge to make one of helium; but children come into the world from the mating of opposites, male and female. A thought made from opposites is always and without exception higher than a thought made from repetition, for it is through the blending of differences, not the multiplication of sameness, that the world is made richer.

All aspects of the difficulties we have experienced in our quest now start to flow smoothly into resolution. Consider what I have just said in terms of the vexed problem of time. The forces of Nature are, in the language of the allegory we have used, aspects of the same desire. The essence of desire is that it looks forward to a goal it has yet to achieve. Thus desire lives in the time it creates. Desire is *becoming*. By contrast, love looks for no reward beyond itself. Love lives *outside time* in the fulfilment that removes the source of its own motivation. Love is *being*.

So what is the climax of this evolution of consciousness, the coda that completes the symphony? When All *becomes* One the cosmos attains a state of absolute consciousness, absolute union. Which means it reaches a state of *absolute love*. But here the paradox on which the world is built asserts itself in its final form. This state of perfection is impossible and cannot last because the very act of reaching absolute being automatically and in consequence denies all acts of past or future becoming.

An allegorical way of showing this is mapped out in Figure 9, which shows the energy of ever more integrated thoughts as waves of increasing amplitude that are symmetric round the crests that mark their highest points. At the limit of the process, the symmetry is abolished altogether and there is no longer a wave. There is a straight line.

Science says the universe began with a 'singularity' of space and time.[136] In so saying, it acknowledges that it is speaking of an impossible state with the energy density of ten trillion galaxies compacted into an imaginary point that has infinite curvative and zero radius. Which brings us to the point of

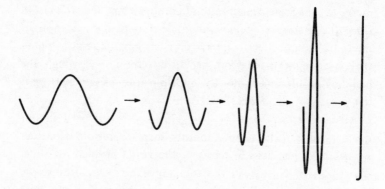

Figure 9 An entirely allegorical way of visualising how one might approach a singularity

the paradox. A paradox unites symmetrically balanced opposites in knowing. But that which is absolute can have no opposite so at the exact instant it comes into 'being' it must dissolve back into 'becoming'. The End must become the Beginning, as T.S. Eliot so truly understood; the wave climax of perfected knowing must explode into the particle chaos of complete ignorance, love must fragment into desire, integration must degenerate into formlessness.

The wave/particle duality that is the essence of the reality paradox holds to the very end/beginning. When the composite wave of completed knowing encompasses All within itself, it has no choice but to 'collapse' into nothing, to start anew on the haunted journey that leads towards the realisation of itself:

> through the unknown, remembered gate
> when the last of earth left to discover
> is that which was the beginning[137]

We can now close the loop for we have returned to the place where we started and perhaps, just perhaps, we can start to know it for the first time.

Nonetheless, a sense of something unfinished lingers. At the start of this book I likened our journey toward the truth to the unwrapping of a present, preparing your mind for the fact that we would have to remove layer after layer to get to the core. Implicit in this metaphor was the concept of *centre*. But where is this centre? What is it?

As ever on this quest science comes to our aid. If we point our telescopes at the night sky we see cities of stars—galaxies— receding from us with a speed proportional to their distance; that is, the farther away they are, the faster they seem to be moving. This seems to position us at the centre of the cosmos, at the fading heart of the fireball. But are we? If we were able to travel to another planet of another sun in another galaxy and repeat this exercise we know that we would get exactly the same result. Once again we would see the galaxies in flight from us, as though the centre had shifted with us, as though *it* moved when *we* moved.[138]

This puzzle is resolved by the understanding that the expanding spacetime bubble is circular. To use a well-worn analogy, the galaxies are like dots painted on the surface of an expanding balloon. As the balloon swells up, the dots move apart, so an observer standing on *any* dot would see *all* other dots as moving away from him. Thus the cosmos is innately democratic; there is no privileged position, all 'points' on the sphere are equal. In yet another revelatory paradox, *the centre is everywhere.*

So we can say, with equal validity, that either there is no centre or the centre is here. Let us opt for the second alternative and, in the spirit of allegory that has animated this journey, consider that this 'point' in space and this 'moment' in time is the centre and that it contains, as many believe, all there is. Joining this allegory to our Christmas box metaphor we can say that, as we peeled away the layers of ignorance that clouded our sight, we have come closer to this 'centre'. In exact proportion, I would argue, we have begun to see more and more clearly the interconnectedness of things. And bit by bit we have approached that vision of wholeness, which is the same as holiness, and the wisdom which was, is and ever shall be true: All is One.

Let us recap what this means in terms of the journey we have shared together. When we began, we saw sight (the world 'out there') as separate from seer (the world 'in here'). That boundary has gone. When we began, we saw one moment as separate from other moments. That boundary has gone. When we began, we saw consciousness as separate from the reality it perceives. That boundary has gone. When we began, we saw the atoms that make up our bodies as separate from the stars that created them. That boundary has gone. When we began, we saw the physics of matter as separate from the physics of morality. That boundary has gone. When we began, we saw one half of a paradox as separate from its partner. That boundary has gone.

The closer we have come to the 'centre', to the point that is everywhere, the more the boundaries that we in our egoic loneliness thought were real have faded into the glimmer of illusion. So where does this process stop? In terms of our metaphor, what is the goal of the journey? What is the truth *inside* the box whose wrappings we have successively removed as we worked our way through our time together? What lives in that universal 'centre', in that holy silence beyond time?

Finally we can begin to see. It is the final and absolute dissolution of *all* boundaries, revealing what, in terms of the spectrum of consciousness, can be called *unitary consciousness*, the One that combines the All. This is why the metaphor of the prism has worked so well, showing as it does how the rainbow of different colours become the one white light of their combined togetherness, how the Many become the One. As the poet Shelley said:

The One remains, the many change and pass;
Heaven's light forever shines, Earth's shadows fly;
Life, like a dome of many-coloured glass,
Stains the white radiance of Eternity.[139]

So at the omnipresent centre, what do we find? Irresistably
and appropriately we find we are left with one perfect, crystal-
clear image—*light*. What is this light? It is the very radiance
of *truth made manifest*; it is the light the poet Walt Whitman
knew, who said of it 'light rare, untellable, lighting the very
light, beyond all signs, descriptions, languages'.[140] This light
beyond light is the radiance of being, the fulfilment of knowing,
analogous to what Buddhists call The Spirit as Ground
(Svabhavikakaya) and encompassing what science is coming to
call *cosmic consciousness*. If we wish to call this 'God' then
that is our privilege, provided we understand that all labels
defile what they seek to define. For the radiance that *is* can
only be known in silence, at the still point of the endless dance,
in the radical simplicity of love.

This is the brightness of knowing that has fired the minds
of the great religious teachers of all ages. This is the light
that came to Gautama under the Bodhi tree in India,
transfiguring his knowing so radically that he became, in the
eyes of his followers, the Buddha or Enlightened One. This
is the light that came to Jesus in the wilderness, expanding
his knowing so wonderfully that he became, in the eyes of
his followers, the Christ or saviour. It is just these moments
of revelation, of illumination, that make up the 'peak
experiences' of the sacred tradition.

And they occur in modern times. In late 1872 a Canadian
psychiatrist R.M. Bucke was travelling in a hansom cab, in
a 'calm and peaceful' frame of mind, when suddenly:

All at once I found myself wrapped in a flame-coloured cloud. For
an instant I thought of fire, an immense conflagration somewhere

close by in that great city; the next, I knew that the fire was within myself. Directly afterward there came upon me a sense of exultation, of immense joyousness accompanied or immediately followed by an intellectual illumination impossible to describe. Among other things, I did not merely come to believe, but I saw that the universe is not composed of dead matter, but is, on the contrary, a living Presence; I was conscious in myself of eternal life. It was not a conviction that I would have eternal life, but a consciousness that I possessed eternal life then . . .[141]

It is a foretaste of this effulgence that NDErs glimpse, in that climactic moment when life falters on the edge of death:

. . . the light just got brighter and brighter and brighter and, it is so bright but it doesn't hurt your eyes, but it's brighter than anything you've ever encountered in your whole life. At that point, I had no consciousness anymore of having a body. It was just pure consciousness. And this enormous bright light seemed almost to cradle me. I just seemed to exist in it and be part of it and be nurtured by it and the feeling just became more and more and more ecstatic and glorious and perfect. And everything about it was—if you took the one thousand best things that ever happened to you in your life and multiplied by a million, maybe you could get close to this feeling . . .[142]

In terms of the musical metaphor that, along with paradox, has structured this text, we can say that this is the music of God pressing from the future into the moment of now. But the songlines of our lives must be *true*, and free of the discordant noise of ego, if they are to blend tunefully with other voices to make the chorus of creation, the one song, in whose beginning was the remembered thought and in whose end the forgotten image.

So our journey ends in the only place it can. In *mystery*! At the root of all things is mystery. Inevitably and without exception. To destroy mystery is to disempower life. Mystery enfolds wonder and wonder is the entrancement of the soul.

When a child looks at the sky in wonder, he sees it as it is. When a man looks at the sky in anticipation of what tomorrow may bring, he sees a reflection of his own needs and desires and because he is smaller in beauty than that which he sees, his seeing is shallower in depth.

So let me bring our time together to a close by looking into this mystery in the spirit of a guided meditation, praying that with this ancient technique I can tell this parable of the End/Beginning in words that will not betray the very truth they seek to capture.

Darkness . . .

A ceaseless movement of dim-glimpsed power . . .

A feeling of immense depth . . .

A change. A dream reaches up from darkness. An awe reaches up to the edge of reality. In the dark of the water, like a shadow glimpsed in a mirror—a mirror of immense depth—is seen something familiar; a premonition aches to become a memory, a wonderment ripples towards an idea . . .

A focusing . . .

And in the Deeps, from the depth, from endlessly far away, a single point of faultless light . . .

Faultless light . . .

Unflawed brightness in which there is no division. The powers that, unchecked, can fashion a world are not separate. An intense brightness, a divine radiance of singular symmetry, like a pearl of perfection lit from within. In this light the balance is not broken, the threshold is not violated. In this brightness that is only self there can be no other. The completed knowing of the universe looks upon itself and sees that it is good . . .

That point of faultless light is the splendour of completed love. It is the brightness that is at the heart of brightness. Unflawed, undivided, seamless, it is the One that is All . . .

All things are One in truth; this means that there can be no separation in truth. This has to be so, for in love which is truth made manifest there is no boundary between being and becoming; they are held in perfect balance as undivided parts of undivided Oneness . . .

Love *is*. Love seeks to go nowhere for it is already at the place of its own fulfilment; it seeks to perform no act for it is, itself, the finished deed of perfect consummation; it is complete, whole, symmetric and absolute.

But truth is always encoded in paradox. And so here, at the very heart of mystery, we find the ultimate paradox. To maintain balance the cosmos must break in the past what it will mend in the future. Remember the rule I showed you from the simple example of a boy's body, or of your own hunger? When the balance is broken, there is desire; where there is desire, there is will-to-action; and where there is will-to-action, there is power! In just this way, love, which is completed being, has to break into desire, which is uncompleted becoming, to remain where it always was. *The balance has to break to remain whole.*

Where is that fracture that cripples being and creates

becoming? When does love 'fall' into desire? In the fulfilled brightness of absolute truth there is no such place and no such moment; rather, that place is everywhere and that moment is everywhen, for in that brightness that is One there can be no separation. But from the perspective of our human eyes there is such a moment, a sharp discontinuity, a point where the balance is shattered. And where the balance is shattered, yes, there is will-to-action and yes, there is desire and yes, there is unbalanced power. And where there is unbalanced power, then—and only then—can the unmanifest be made manifest in the upwelling Act of Creation.

The breaking of the balance is the instant of Creation, the point where eternity stops and time begins.

But we are only halfway through this paradox. The thing that drives desire is its yearning to be whole, the torment of brokenness can only be healed in the ecstasy of union. So the very act of breaking that begins the world brings forth the wisdom needed to swing it on an upward arc, back to the undivided love that made it, the love which, in truth, it has never left.

The fact of separation brings into being the promise of reunion. In exact measure. The fact of separation creates the desire to be whole. In exact measure. It is as though the two halves of a paradox which, when understood, reconcile their own opposites in perfect harmony, split apart. From this breaking ignorance is born, and incompleteness, a sense of something unfinished. No longer is life forever born through the ongoing act of perpetual dying, no, now the becoming of life is separated from the ending of death. *Time is made manifest.*

But time has about it a strangeness that will puzzle us for as long as we remain human. What is this thing called time? Where is time? How can you reckon time in the brightness of eternity where fifteen billion years of human time become a phantom moment on a clock that keeps no count?

In the truth of the brightness, love is forever dissolving into desire to be forever restored to its own perfection by a perpetual act of consummative union. The brightness is alive with this creative tension. In the brightness the riddle of being and becoming is reconciled in one transcendent sweep of all-encompassing consciousness. But minds that are not complete in their knowing can see this love only in bits, one after the other. So in their hunger for eternity, they get *ensnared in time*; in their quest for love, they get seduced by desire; in their search for being, they trap themselves in *becoming*.

This is the trap of humanity which, in the broken shards of time, chases the moving shadow of an eternal love it *already possesses*.

I believe it is that simple.

Chapter 13

---

phase transition

The motif of the last chapter was the paradox that we must reach the end to know the beginning. That was a generic statement. I now want to make it personal. My own journey began with a crisis of meaning brought on by illness and by a confrontation with death. In this closing chapter I want to share with you the way I have resolved this crisis for myself, in the hope that it may help resolve aspects of it for you.

Let me live out the metaphor that 'in my end is my beginning' by returning to a starting point of this book. In the Introduction I showed Figure 1 as 'ending' with consciousness. By which I mean the average structure of consciousness as it is represented in most of us at this moment. But we have seen that this is impossible. As Chapter 11 showed, *there is nothing special about this moment in evolutionary time apart from the fact that we happen to inhabit it.* So there is absolutely nothing, in logic or commonsense, that tells us that evolution has reached its zenith in the present structure of the human mind. Just the reverse! Unless we bring the evolutionary experiment to a halt here on earth, I believe our species will inevitably go through a transfiguration so profound that we, the parents of the change, will not even recognise the child we are giving birth to.

Our old software tends to reject this, so let me make two points about the way evolution works. If we look at human history in the wider perspective of what we may call 'deep time', one gets the impression that evolution is somehow tracking a trajectory of ever-accelerating change. What this means becomes clear if we reduce the 3.5 billion-year history of life on earth to a 24-hour timescale (see Figure 10) and set the origin of life at noon. On this reduced scale, plants only invade the land at 8.00 p.m.; the age of reptiles does not begin until 9.40 p.m.; humans first appear at 11.59 p.m.; recorded history starts at a quarter of a second before midnight. Thus there is a strong sense that the pace of change increases with time so that the intervals between major landmarks, major modes of being, get shorter and shorter as the process unfolds. To put it technically, evolution trends towards exponential kinetics.

Many people expect evolutionary change to be gradual and linear. But much change in nature is rapid and nonlinear. Take a simple physical system—a glass of water which is being progressively cooled, one degree at a time. As we go from 11°C to 10°C there is no visible change in the character of the system. Ditto for the change from 4°C to 3°C, 3°C to 2°C, 2°C to 1°C. But the change from 1°C to 0°C changes everything; there occurs what scientists call a phase transition—a sudden dramatic shift in the properties of the entire system.

Note that, numerically, the temperature drop between 1°C and 0°C is no greater than any of the drops which preceded it. But the consequences of that 1 to 0 drop are all-encompassing. Note, too, that the moment a phase transition occurs is exactly that moment when, unbeknown to outside observers, the system is inwardly 'teetering on the brink'. At such a pivot-point it takes but a tiny push, provided it is applied in the right place, to change everything.

The History of Life on a 24-Hour Scale

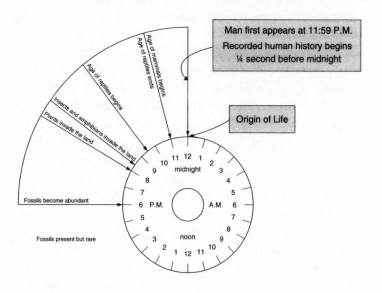

Figure 10 Evolution appears to track what mathematicians call exponential kinetics. The intervals between the major 'landmarks' appear to get shorter and shorter with time. Note that one cannot give any scientifically acceptable interpretation of this apparent tendency because we have no yardstick with which we can measure the complexity of an object. We may feel certain that a gazelle represents a 'higher' level of organisation than a star but we cannot quantify this parameter in a meaningful way.

My belief is that *we, as a species, are teetering on the brink of a phase transition right now*, one that involves a transfiguration not of matter but of mind. Unfortunately one cannot be specific about a change that is going on behind the very eyes that are looking for it but I am convinced that it will track the theme I have tried to map out in this book—the path of increasing integration that is the hallmark of deepening awareness.

I have introduced the concept of a phase transition because the moments of truly deep integration which I have highlighted through the course of this book—integrations in depth that reveal All to be One—typically occur with the suddenness of a phase transition 'in a flash,' 'out of the blue'. These moments are not hypothetical fancies; they have happened throughout history to those individuals whose transfigured consciousness has shaped the destiny of the human race. Such an illuminating moment came to an Indian prince Gautama Siddhartha, sitting under a Bodhi tree in India; to a Nazarene, Jesus, in the wilderness of Israel, to the Roman Plotinus, to Julian of Norwich and Hildegard of Bingen, to Dante, Blake, Spinoza and to Walt Whitman lying in the grass of his beloved America. These are the 'peak experiences' of the mystical tradition and their defining feature is the holism of the vision that they deliver with such overpowering clarity.[143]

How can we get inside the cognitive space of a peak experience? The answer is, we cannot, for the insight by its very nature is untellable in any words. All I can do is present you with something that has worked for me, the description of such a revelatory moment that occurs as the climax of Somerset Maugham's novel, *The Razor's Edge*. While the character in question is fictional, his experience is not—it is clearly derived from the kind of experience the Canadian physician R.M. Bucke collates in his definitive text, *Cosmic Consciousness*.[144]

I was ravished with the beauty of the world. I'd never known such exultation and such a transcendent joy . . . I felt as though I was suddenly released from my body and as pure spirit partook of a loveliness I had never conceived. I had a sense that a knowledge more than human possessed me, so that everything that had been confused was clear and everything that had perplexed me was explained. I was so happy that it was pain and I struggled to release myself from it for I felt that if it lasted a moment longer I should die; and yet it was such rapture that I was ready to die rather than forego it. How can I tell you what I felt?[145]

Anyone unused to the language of the mystical tradition will probably find this description 'over the top' and thus perhaps lacking in credibility. But listen to the parallel words of one of the greatest scientists of our time, Albert Einstein:

The most beautiful thing we can experience is the mysterious. It is the source of all true art and science. He who can no longer wonder or stand rapt in awe is as good as dead, a snuffed out candle . . . To know that what is impenetrable to our senses really exists, manifesting itself as the most profound wisdom and most radiant beauty, which our dull faculties can comprehend only in their most primitive forms, this knowledge, this feeling, is the centre of true religion.[146]

Many people allow the possibility of a state of 'expanded consciousness' or 'cosmic consciousness' in individuals but deny it has any relevance to the collective evolution of our species. They say, correctly, that the insights provided by the visionaries of the sacred tradition have not been understood; they have been misunderstood and the fruits of this misunderstanding are responsible for what is going on at this very moment, in Bosnia and Northern Ireland. As Evelyn Underhill aptly said, 'it has been the tragedy of the founder of every great religion to have had re-erected in their wakes the very barriers they laboured to cast down'.[147]

In evolutionary terms, the defining feature of an advantageous 'mutant' quality is that it spreads through the population until, eventually, it becomes the common property of the species and what was once rare becomes the norm. If humanity were evolving towards a higher state of consciousness we might expect to see more evidence of it. Instead, a cynic might well argue, we see less.

One of the most significant changes that has come over my own thinking in the past decade is the realisation that this cynical conclusion is not just misplaced but the wrong way round. What we see in the world today is exactly *what we would expect of a species in transition*, negotiating the difficult passage from one mode of being to another. For it is a defining feature of any profound transformation that it involves *ordeal*, it involves *suffering* and—here is where it takes me back to the start of my own journey—it often involves illness.

I want to bring this book to a close by looking at this issue from two intertwined points of view, seeking first for evidence that such higher consciousness is becoming more common and, second, for the crisis that makes its emergence possible.

Where is the evidence for an increasing frequency of heightened consciousness in a world which seems to be degrading the quality of its compassion with every day that passes? My example—the near-death experience or NDE—has already been dealt with in depth. When I first 'discovered' this phenomenon, my own scientific 'software' tempted me to put it in the same 'fringe' category as UFOs and poltergeists. But the clinical facts are too well documented and I am now convinced that, whatever the interpretation, the phenomenon itself is real. What excited me, as I began to explore the subject, was that the experience these people reported was to me and to at least one researcher of the subject, Professor Kenneth Ring of the University of Connecticut, precisely the same ineffable experience that runs through much of the world's great poetry and through its sacred writings down the ages.[148]

To detail the comparison as I have come to see it I need only emphasise or recap the material dealt with in Chapter 9. Listen to Paul, who was electrocuted in 1972:

> While I stood in the light, for that split second or split seconds or few minutes, whatever it was in time, I had this feeling of just total understanding. It was just being part of that universal spirit, part of what you can only describe as being all. Everything—you know—positive and negative—and it was the most inspiring and, I guess, the greatest single experience I have ever had in my life. It was just incredible.[149]

Here, in the halting words of an ordinary man, is that same deep sense of the oneness of things, the conviction that All is One, which, to me, defines the evolution of consciousness.

Not only the sense of unity, but all the elements of the mystical insight are here, in the NDE: ineffable light, transcendent love, an intuition of timelessness, the loss of the sense of self. Compare the sensations of timelessness detailed in Chapter 9 with this tiny sample of the world's mystical literature that expresses just this insight:

> Time out of mind my journey
> circles the universe
> and I remain
> before the first day.[150]

> Time past and time future
> what might have been and what has been
> point to one end, which is always present.[151]

> Before Abraham was, I am.[152]

Note that the argument I am adopting does not require us to stake out any position about what the NDE 'means'. The implications of the NDE for any possible survival of consciousness after death are less important for my theme than the *transformative effects* it has on the psychology of those who live through it. Detailed analyses of the after-effects of the NDE[153] confirm the pioneering findings of Kenneth Ring, Margot Grey and others, that survivors of the NDE are permanently changed in just the way we would expect of individuals whose consciousness has been taken outside the norms. If their transformations seem less profound than those undergone by a Jesus or a Dante or a Whitman, that, too, is understandable. These people had, for the most part, not been on a preparatory spiritual journey; they had been prematurely shocked into a higher state of consciousness by a sudden encounter with physical death. What matters is that the after-effects of that brief encounter are real and permanent, that they point in exactly the direction we would expect— towards greater caring, a lessened regard for material things, a desire to be of service to others, a more integrated awareness.

I will now try and draw the various threads of my argument together into one final statement. As I said at the beginning, by a paradox that is somehow fittingly inevitable, I have come to believe that science—the agent that once removed a sense of the sacred from life—has become, at least in part, the agent that restores it. Not merely because its own insights are enriching and extending those of the sacred traditions but because the technology it has spawned is allowing large numbers of people to enter states of expanded consciousness that have previously been the preserve of the very few. The common and increasingly survivable encounter with physical death is opening a window into the deeps of the human mind that hitherto only opened for the pioneers of the psycho-spiritual journey, the explorers who consciously sought 'the death of the self'; understanding the price it carries, as I have already specified it and as T.S. Eliot knew it to be: 'a condition of complete simplicity, costing not less than everything'.

For many readers the concept that we are evolving into a higher state of consciousness probably seems romantic, impossible, pie-in-the-sky. But to think this way is to ignore the whole message of evolution. Seventy million years ago we were small creatures not much bigger than rats, scuttling through the trees of long-vanished forests. Now we make music and fly to the moon. So to argue against the inevitable emergence of phases of being that are superior to ours is to deny the universe the creative capacity that has already brought forth, in succession, electrons, atoms, stars, ammonites, crocodiles, humans and the ability to marvel at the stupendous artistry to which the whole process bears witness.

This is science's priceless gift; we need no longer regard ourselves as accidental irrelevancies in a mechanical universe but as participating co-creators of what, at the beginning of this book, I called an *evolving work of art*. Brian Swimme captures the mood of my meaning perfectly when he says, 'We are coming to understand that the universe was [sic] aiming towards a space where it could reflect upon itself in conscious self-awareness and that the human is precisely that space'.[154]

But we must never forget the price evolution asks of us for any act of transcendence. The dark side of the equation is that growth is coupled to suffering by links that cannot be severed. I believe that we have to start to see sickness in the light of the principle highlighted in Chapter 11, understanding that, despite New Age protestations to the contrary, transcendence and pain are as indissolubly interknit as creation and destruction, good and bad, up and down.

Jung was one of the first to understand that a person presenting for therapy is, at the root level, often engaged in an existentialist crisis—a crisis of *meaning*. This has been my theme and my experience. While people see life as pointless, while they feel helpless victims of circumstances they cannot control, then we will see around us exactly what we see today, whether we look at the violated landscape without or the violated landscape within, for the one is the mirror of the other.

How does the message of science help us? Again I turn to the concept of a phase transition. There are two features of a phase transition that bear upon our present moment. A phase transition is always a crisis because the tension it embodies can be resolved in one of two ways; either a system can use the dark energy of breakdown to transcend its own prior limitations or the system can collapse upon itself. A system's phase transition is thus precisely its own near-death moment—that moment of critical climax when its reality is challenged at its very roots. The two are one and the same.

The French biologist Jacques Monod said of our moment that neither our duty nor our destiny have been written down.[155] I believe that. I do not for one solitary second accept the New Age guarantee that says the universe will look after us. We saw earlier that individual songlines select themselves into or out of higher states of consciousness according to the quality of the music that they make. In just this fashion a crisis of collective consciousness is also a 'fitness trial', a test of our confederate worthiness to inherit the future. If, through our own indifference or our own greed, the evolutionary experiment fails on this planet, the torch of evolving consciousness will be picked up elsewhere, on some other planet round some other sun.

This may seem a threatening thought but it brings me to the second feature of a phase transition, the one I wish to close on. As I have already said, a phase transition, like any deep crisis, is precisely the moment when the entire system teeters on the brink; at that moment, it takes but the tiniest flicker of energy, to push the system into collapse or transcendence, to change it irredeemably and forever.

What does this mean for us 'here and now'? It means that *what we do as individuals matters*. Really matters. Balanced as we are on an evolutionary knife-edge, the actions of each one of us can have repercussions beyond our capacity to imagine. Because we do not understand the physics of consciousness we do not understand how the insights of the one might affect the 'critical mass' of the whole. But we do not stand alone, we are all interlinked. This is the message of this book and my deepest conviction—*All is One*. This is the convergent message of both science and the sacred sense. So each time we make a choice that puts self ahead of other, each time we withhold a word of compassion from a troubled friend, we shift the balance, albeit perhaps slightly, towards our collective extinction. By contrast, each time we smile at someone in the street, each time we extend a caring hand to a fellow creature in distress, we move—*all of us*—towards that light which illuminates the near-death moment with love.

I would like to leave you with a quote from an American ecologist John Robbins[156] that captures the mood of the dangerous opportunity offered by this planetary near-death experience we are all living through:

> This sorrow belongs to us all, and I have learned it is not something to fear. For in the depths of our shared pain we also experience our shared caring . . . and our common capacity to act. The pain we feel is the cracking of the shell that encloses our power to respond. Something precious can be born in times like these. In our shared pain we labour together to bring it to birth . . .
>
> Obviously the work of healing our world and ourselves is not a separate or passing chapter in our lives. The changes that are necessary won't come about simply because we stop eating meat, or simply because, on occasion, we meet or march or donate or lobby. It will take everything we are, and it will take all of us, and in forms we cannot yet even begin to imagine . . .
>
> I look out into the world and I see a deep night of unthinkable cruelty and blindness. Undaunted, however, I look within the human heart and find something of love there, something that cares and shines out into the dark universe like a bright beacon.

And in the shining of that light within, I feel the dreams and prayers of all beings. In the shining of that beacon I feel all of our hopes for a better future. In the shining of the human heartlight there is the strength to do what must be done.

Each moment is an undiscovered country.

1 McLean, Don © 1971 copyright MCA Inc/Mayday-Media Arts Music. All rights reserved. Used by permission.
2 Reanney, Darryl C. (1991) *The Death of Forever*, Longman Cheshire, Melbourne.
3 Whittier, John Greenleaf (undated 19th century edn) 'My Triumph' in *The Poetical Works of John Greenleaf Whittier*, W.P. Nimmo, Hay & Mitchell, Edinburgh.
4 Malouf, David (1978) *An Imaginary Life*, Chatto & Windus, London.
5 Eliot, T.S. (1969) *The Complete Poems and Plays*, Faber & Faber, London.
6 *The Creation of Ea* (source unknown).
7 Wilber, Ken (1985) *No Boundary*, Shambhala, New York.
8 Davies, Paul (1992a) *The Mind of God*, Simon & Schuster, New York.
9 Sagan, Carl (1977) *The Dragons of Eden*, Hodder & Stoughton, London.
10 Penrose, Roger (1989) *The Emperor's New Mind: Concerning Computers, Minds and the Laws of Physics*, Oxford University Press, Oxford.

11 Kuhn, Thomas (1962) *The Structure of Scientific Revolutions*, Chicago University Press, Chicago.
12 Bohm, David in *New Scientist*, 27 February, 1993.
13 Hadamard, Jacques (1945) *The Psychology of Invention in the Mathematical Field*, Princeton University Press, Princeton.
14 Malouf, D. (1978).
15 Weinberg, Steven (1977) *The First Three Minutes*, Andre Deutsch, London.
16 Berrill, N.J. (1958) *You and the Universe*, Dodd, Mead & Co., New York.
17 Swimme, Brian (1984) *The Universe is a Green Dragon*, Bear & Co., Santa Fe.
18 Reanney, D. (1991).
19 ibid.
20 ibid.
21 Davies, Paul (1992b) on *Lateline*, ABC Television, Australia.
22 Eliot, Alexander (1990) *The Universal Myths*, Miridian, New York.
23 Weyl, Hermann (1989) *Symmetry*, Princeton University Press, Princeton.
24 Hawking, Stephen W. (1988) *A Brief History of Time*, Bantam, London.
25 Davies, Paul (1984) *Superforce*, Heinemann, London.
26 ibid.
27 Fitzgerald, Edward (trans.) (1961) *The Rubaiyat of Omar Khayyam*, A. & C. Black, London.
28 Einstein, Albert (1920) *Relativity*, Methuen, London. See also many popular books on the subject, e.g. John Gribbin, *In Search of the Big Bang*, Heinemann, London, 1987.
29 ibid.
30 Reanney, D. (1991) and Wilber, K. (1985).
31 It is necessary to specify that the hypothetical consciousness at issue is 'disembodied' because no material body can accelerate to the speed of light.

32 An excellent popular account of Einstein's 'thought experiment' in this regard is to be found in J. Bronowski, *The Ascent of Man*, BBC Books, London, 1974.

33 Einstein, A. (1920).

34 Davies, P. (1984).

35 Raine, Kathleen (1956) *Collected Poems*, Hamish Hamilton, London.

36 Reanney, D. (1991).

37 Reanney, Darryl C. (1972) *Life's Language*, Associated Book Publishers, Sydney.

38 Reanney, D. (1991).

39 Blakemore, Colin (1988) *The Mind Machine*, BBC Books, London.

40 Ornstein, Robert (1986) *Multimind*, Macmillan, London.

41 Furst, Charles (1979) *Origins of the Mind: Mind-Brain Connections*, Prentice-Hall, Englewood Cliffs, New Jersey.

42 Graves, Robert (1962) *The Unnamed Spell: New Poems*, Cassell, London.

43 Gribbin, John (1984) *In Search of Schroedinger's Cat*, Wildwood, London; Davies, Paul (1988) *Other Worlds*, Penguin, UK.

44 Gribbin, J. (1984).

45 John Wheeler quoted in Fritjof Capra, *The Tao of Physics*, Wildwood House, London, 1975.

46 Swimme, Brian (1990) *Feast of Consciousness: Canticle to the Cosmos* (video series), Newstory Project, San Francisco.

47 Gribbin, J. (1984).

48 Cambell, Joseph (1988) *The Masks of God*, Viking, UK.

49 Eliot, T.S. (1969).

50 Malouf, D. (1978).

51 Hopkins, Gerard Manley (1956) *Poems and Prose of Gerard Manley Hopkins*, Penguin, UK.

52 Gribbin, J. (1984).

53 Gribbin, J. (1984) and Davies, P. (1988).

54 No one has ever taken a 'show of hands' on this subject

but my reading of the situation is that most physicists, while admitting the unsettling nature of the quantum revelation, are reluctant to give mind a crucial role in the scheme of things.

55 du Nouy, Lecomte (1946) *Human Destiny*, Longmans Green, London.
56 Penrose, R. (1989).
57 Bohm, David (1951) *Quantum Theory*, Constable, UK.
58 Zohar, Danah (1990) *The Quantum Self*, Bloomsbury, London.
59 Wilber, K. (1985).
60 Huxley, Aldous (1946) *The Perennial Philosophy*, Chatto & Windus, London.
61 Talbot, Michael (1991) *The Holographic Universe*, HarperCollins, New York.
62 See, for example, Mary Lutyens (ed.), *The Krishnamurti Reader*, Arkana, UK.
63 ibid.
64 Sheldrake, Rupert (1985) *A New Science of Life: the Hypothesis of Formative Causation*, Blond & Briggs, London.
65 *Insight into One*, unscreened interview between the author and His Holiness, the 14th Dalai Lama, Melbourne, 4 May 1992, Vixen Films Pty Ltd.
66 Hadamard, J. (1945).
67 Penrose, R. (1989).
68 In physics, a 'standing wave' may be set up whenever a wave vibrating between two fixed points is exactly divided by sets of whole numbers.
69 Renault, Mary (1972) *The Persian Boy*, Longman, London.
70 Rucker, Rudy (1982) *Infinity and the Mind*, Birkhauser, Boston.
71 Penrose, R. (1989).
72 Davies, P. (1992a).
73 Gleick, James (1988) *Chaos*, Heinemann, London.
74 Penrose, R. (1989).
75 One can interpret this statement in terms of Sheldrake's

concept of 'morphic resonance' (see Rupert Sheldrake, *The Presence of the Past*, Collins, London, 1988) but other, perhaps simpler, explanations are possible.

76 Penrose, R. (1989).

77 DeValois, K.K., DeValois, R.L. and Yund, W.W. (1979) 'Responses of Striate Cortex Cells to Grating and Checkerboard Patterns' in *Journal of Physiology*, No. 291.

78 See, for example, Talbot, M. (1991).

79 Penrose, R. (1989).

80 Gribbin, J. (1984).

81 Hasluck, N. (1990) *The Country Without Music*, Viking, Melbourne.

82 Maybury-Lewis, David (1992) *Millenium*, Viking, New York.

83 Chatwin, Bruce (1987) *The Songlines*, Picador, UK.

84 Shakespeare, William *Measure for Measure*, 3:1.

85 Browning, Robert, 'Prospice'. See for example *The Poems of Robert Browning* (1928) Oxford University Press, Oxford.

86 Shakespeare, William *Hamlet*, 3:1.

87 Davies, P. (1988).

88 Grey, Margot (1987) *Return from Death*, Arkana, UK.

89 Moody, Raymond (1977) *Life after Life*, Bantam, New York.

90 ibid.

91 Ring, Kenneth (1985) *Heading towards Omega*, William Morrow, New York.

92 Ring, Kenneth (1991) 'Amazing Grace: the Near-Death Experience as a Compensatory Gift' in *Journal of Near-Death Studies*, Human Sciences Press, New York, Vol. 10, No. 1.

93 Ring, K. (1985).

94 ibid.

95 Fremantle, F. and Trungpa, C. (1987) *The Tibetan Book of the Dead* Shambhala, New York.

96 Sagan, Carl (1979) 'The Amniotic Universe' in *Broca's Brain*, Hodder & Stoughton, London.

97 Lorimer, David (1990) *Whole in One*, Arkana, UK.

98 Ring, K. (1985).

99 ibid.

100 Lorimer, D. (1990).

101 ibid.

102 ibid.

103 Ring, K. (1991).

104 Eliot, T.S. (1969).

105 Wren-Lewis, John (1992) in *The Couchman Series*, ABC Television, Australia.

106 Ring, Kenneth (1990) 'Shamanic Initiation, Imaginal Worlds and Light after Death' in Gary Doore (ed.) *What Survives?* J.P. Tarcher Inc., Los Angeles.

107 Cambell, Joseph (1990) *Transformations of Myth through Time*, Harper & Row, New York.

108 Eliot, T.S. (1969).

109 Fremantle, F. and Trungpa, C. (1987).

110 Atwater, Phyllis (1988) *Coming back to Life*, Collins Dove, Melbourne.

111 Moody, R. (1977).

112 Ring, K. (1985).

113 Wren-Lewis, J. (1992).

114 For a fascinating but highly speculative account see Fred Alan Wolf, *Parallel Universes*, Touchstone, New York, 1990.

115 See, for example, G. Seldes, *The Great Quotations*, Castle Books, New Jersey, 1960.

116 Moody, R. (1977).

117 Whitman, Walt (n.d.) *Leaves of Grass*, Modern Library, New York.

118 Swimme, Brian (1990) *The Story of Our Time: Canticle to the Cosmos* (video series), Newstory Project, San Francisco.

119 Wilber, K. (1985).

120 See, for example, R. Heffner, H. Rehder and W. Twaddel *Goethe's Faust*, D.C. Heath & Co., Boston, 1954.

121 Harvey, Andrew (1991) *Hidden Journey*, Bloomsbury, London.

122 Davies, P. (1984).

123 Eliot, T.S. (1969).

124 Reanney, D. (1991).

125 Davies, Paul (1987) *The Accidental Universe*, Cambridge University Press, Cambridge.

126 Swimme, Brian (1991) *The Nature of the Human: Canticle to the Cosmos* (video series), Newstory Project, San Francisco.

127 de Chardin, Teilhard (1965) *The Phenomenon of Man*, Collins, London.

128 Darling, D (1989) *Deep Time*, Bantam, New York.

129 Readers have a right to ask what I mean by this. I am referring to the many documented examples of supposedly 'paranormal' occurrences which appear to support the notion that mind can affect matter to a degree that goes beyond the laws of physics. Almost all of this evidence is anecdotal, hence suspect in the eyes of science. I offer one example from personal experience. A young man under hypnosis was told that the potato he held in his hand was an apple. From that moment on, until the 'spell' was lifted, he looked at the potato and saw an apple, and he became angry at attempts to explain that he was hallucinating. Our commonsense approach to this is that the potato was 'real' and the apple an 'illusion' implanted in the youth's mind by the hypnotist. But what if the group of witnesses had been collectively hypnotised to regard the potato as an apple so that the *consensual reality* deviated from the version of reality which we, in our wider experiential framework, accept as valid? Anyone familiar with hypnosis can probably think of similar examples, suggesting that the structure of our 'reality' is a very fragile construct indeed.

130 Raine, K. (1956).

131 Rucker, Rudy (1986) *The Fourth Dimension*, Penguin, UK.

132 Star, J. (1991) *Two Suns Rising: a collection of sacred writing*, Bantam, New York.

133 ibid.

134 Darling, D. (1989).

135 Swimme, Brian and Berry, Thomas (1992) *The Universe Story*, HarperCollins, New York.

136 Davies, P. (1984).

137 Eliot, T.S. (1969).

138 Hawking, S. (1988).

139 See, for example, *Selected Poems of Percy Bysshe Shelley*, Oxford University Press, Oxford, 1964.

140 Whitman, W. *Leaves of Grass*.

141 Bucke, Richard M. (1962) *Cosmic Consciousness*, E.P. Dutton & Co., New York.

142 Ring, K. (1985).

143 See, for example, Anne Bancroft, *The Luminous Vision*, Allen & Unwin, London, 1982.

144 Bucke, R. (1962).

145 Maugham, W. Somerset (1955) *The Razor's Edge*, The Vanguard Library, London.

146 Einstein, Albert in *I Believe: Nineteen Personal Philosophies*, Allen & Unwin, London (n.d.).

147 Johnson, Raynor C. (1957) *The Imprisoned Splendour*, Hodder & Stoughton, London.

148 Ring, K. (1985).

149 Elder, Bruce (1987) *And When I Die Will I Be Dead?* ABC Enterprises, Sydney.

150 Raine, K. (1956).

151 Eliot, T.S. (1969).

152 New Testament.

153 See, for example, Cherie Sutherland, *Transformed by the Light*, Bantam, Sydney, 1992.

154 Swimme, B. (1991) *The Nature of the Human.*

155 Monod, Jacques (1971) *Chance and Necessity*, Collins, London.

156 Robbins, John (1987) *Diet for a New America*, Stillpoint, Walpole, New Hampshire.

Some of the books which have had some input, directly or indirectly, into *Music of the Mind* are listed below in categories to facilitate ease of reference. With a few exceptions, only accessible 'non-technical' books have been listed. Many of the categories overlap so, in some cases, the same book is represented in two or more categories.

Cosmology and the origin and evolution of the universe
Abell, G. (1969) *Exploration of the Universe*, 2nd edn, Holt, Rinehart & Winston, New York.
Barrow, J. (1991) *Theories of Everything*, Vintage, London.
Barrow, J. and Silk, J. (1984) *The Left Hand of Creation*, Unwin, London.
Berrill, N. (1958) *You and the Universe*, Dodd, Mead & Co., New York.
Darling, D. (1989) *Deep Time*, Bantam, New York.
Davies, P. (1983) *God and the New Physics*, Dent & Sons, London.
Davies, P. (1984) *Superforce*, Heinemann, London.

Davies, P. (1987) *The Accidental Universe*, Cambridge University Press, Cambridge.

Davies, P. (1987) *The Cosmic Blueprint*, Heinemann, London.

Davies, P. (1988) *Other Worlds*, Dent & Sons, London.

Davies, P. and Gribbin, J. (1991) *The Matter Myth*, Viking, London.

Gribbin, J. (1987) *In Search of the Big Bang*, Heinemann, London.

Gribbin, J. (1987) *The Omega Point*, Heinemann, London.

Gribbin, J. and Rees, M. (1990) *Cosmic Coincidences*, Heinemann, London.

Hinkelbein, A. (1972) *Origins of the Universe*, Verlag, J.F. Schreiber, Esslingen.

Jastrow, R. and Thompson, M. (1972) *Astronomy, Fundamentals and Frontiers*, 2nd edn, Wiley and Sons, New York.

Kraus, L. (1990) *The Fifth Essence*, Hutchinson Radius, London.

Layzer, D. (1990) *Cosmogenesis*, Oxford University Press, Oxford.

Pagels, H. (1983) *The Cosmic Code*, Michael Joseph, London.

Pagels, H. (1985) *Perfect Symmetry*, Simon & Schuster, New York.

Swimme, B. and Berry, T. (1992) *The Universe Story*, HarperCollins, New York.

Weinberg, S. (1977) *The First Three Minutes*, Andre Deutsch, London.

The nature of time

Barnett, L. (1949) *The Universe and Dr Einstein*, Collins, London.

Blum, H. (1951) *Time's Arrow and Evolution*, Princeton University Press, Princeton.

Coveny, P. and Highfield, R. (1990) *The Arrow of Time*, W.H. Allen, London.

Darling, D. (1989) *Deep Time*, Bantam, New York.

Durrell, C. (1926) *Readable Relativity*, G. Bell & Sons, London.

Einstein, A. (1920) *Relativity*, Methuen, London.

Fraser, J. (1987) *Time, the Familiar Stranger*, Tempus Books, Washington.

Hawking, S. (1988) *A Brief History of Time*, Bantam, London.

Reanney, D. (1991) *The Death of Forever*, Longman Cheshire Melbourne.

Whitrow, G. (1988) *Time in History*, Oxford University Press, Oxford.

Zohar, D. (1990) *Through the Time Barrier*, Heinemann, London.

Quantum mechanics

Barrow, J. (1988) *The World within the World*, Oxford University Press, Oxford.

Davies, P. (1980) *Other Worlds*, Dent & Sons, London.

Gribbin, J. (1984) *In Search of Schroedinger's Cat*, Wildwood, London.

Hoffmann, B. (1947) *The Strange Story of the Quantum*, Penguin, UK.

Polkinghorne, J. (1984) *The Quantum World*, Longman, London.

Swimme, B. (1990) *Canticle to the Cosmos* video series, Newstory Project, San Francisco.

Brain biology and the nature of consciousness

Bergson, H. (1988) *Matter and Memory* (translated by N.M. Paul and W. Scott Palmer), Zone Books, New York.

Blakemore, C. (1988) *The Mind Machine*, BBC Books, London.

Dennett, D. (1991) *Consciousness Explained*, Little Brown & Co., Boston.

Grof, S. (1985) *Beyond the Brain*, State University of New York, New York.

Magouin, H. (1958) *The Waking Brain*, Charles C. Thomas, Illinois.

Ornstein, R. (1986) *Multimind*, Macmillan, London.

Penrose, R. (1989) *The Emperor's New Mind*, Oxford University Press, Oxford.

Restak, R. (1984) *The Brain*, Educational Broadcasting Corporation, Bantam, Toronto.

Rosenfield, W.E. (1992) *The Strange, familiar and forgotten: an anatomy of consciousness*, Alfred A. Knopf, New York.

Sagan, C. (1977) *The Dragons of Eden*, Hodder & Stoughton, London.

Zohar, D. (1990) *The Quantum Self*, Bloomsbury, London.

Dying and the near-death experience

Atwater, P. (1988) *Coming Back to Life*, Collins Dove, Melbourne.

Doore, G. (ed.) (1990) *What Survives?* J.P. Tarcher Inc., Los Angeles.

Elder, B. (1987) *And When I Die Will I Be Dead?* ABC Enterprises, Sydney.

Enright, D. (1983) *The Oxford Book of Death*, Oxford University Press, Oxford.

Freemantle, F. and Trungpa, C. (trans.) (1987) *The Tibetan Book of the Dead*, Shambhala, New York.

Grey, M. (1987) *Return From Death*, Arkana, UK.

Hick, J. (1976) *Death and Eternal Life*, Collins & Sons, Glasgow.

Kramer, K. (1988) *The Sacred Art of Dying*, Paulist Press, New York.

Kübler-Ross, E. (1969) *On Death and Dying*, Macmillan, New York.

Kübler-Ross, E. (1974) *Questions on Death and Dying*, Macmillan, New York.

Kübler-Ross, E. (1975) *Death, the Final Stage of Growth*, Touchstone, New York.

Levine, S. (1982) *Who Dies?* Anchor Doubleday, New York.

Lorimar, D. (1990) *Whole in One*, Arkana, London.

Moody, R. (1977) *Life after Life*, Bantam, New York.

Moody, R. (1977) *Reflections on Life after Life*, Bantam, New York.

Nathan, J. (1992) *Time of My Life*, Penguin, Melbourne.

Reed, E. (1970) *Helping Children with the Mystery of Death*, Abingdon, Nashville.

Ring, K. (1980) *Life at Death*, William Morrow, New York.

Ring, K. (1985) *Heading Towards Omega*, William Morrow, New York.

Ring, K. (1992) *The Omega Project*, William Morrow, New York.

Sutherland, C. (1992) *Transformed by the Light*, Bantam, New York.

Taylor, A. (1989) *Acquainted with the Night*, Fontana, London.

The future of consciousness

Bucke, R. (1962) *Cosmic Consciousness*, E.P. Dutton & Co, New York.

Darling, D. (1989) *Deep Time*, Bantam, New York.

Davies, P. (1992) *The Mind of God*, Simon & Schuster, New York.

Grof, S. (1992) *The Holotropic Mind*, Harper, San Francisco.

Jahn, R. and Dunne, B. (1987) *Margins of Reality*, Harvest HBJ, San Diego.

Peat, F.D. (1991) *The Philosopher's Stone*, Bantam, New York.

Reanney, D. (1991) *The Death of Forever*, Longman Cheshire, Melbourne.

Ring, K. (1985) *Heading Towards Omega*, William Morrow, New York.

Talbot, M. (1991) *The Holographic Universe*, HarperCollins, New York.

Wallace, B. (1989) *Choosing Reality*, Shambhala, New York.

Wilber, K. (1985) *No Boundary*, Random Century, New York.

The sacred traditions

Bancroft, A. (1982) *The Luminous Vision*, Allen & Unwin, London.

Brunton, P. (1969) *The Wisdom of the Overself*, Weiser, York Beach.

du Nouy, L. (1946) *Human Destiny,* Longmans Green, London.

Easwaran, D. (1986) *The Dhammapada*, Arkana, UK.

Easwaran, D. (1987) *The Upanishads*, Arkana, UK.

Edwards, D. (1992) *Made from Stardust*, Collins Dove, Melbourne.

Heinberg, R. (1989) *Memories and Visions of Paradise*, Aquarian Press, Wellingborough, UK.

Huxley, A. (1946) *The Perennial Philosophy*, Chatto & Windus, London.

Jung, C. (1964) *Man and His Symbols*, Aldus Books, London.

Maybury-Lewis, D. (1992) *Millenium*, Viking, New York.

O'Conner, P. (1985) *Understanding Jung*, Methuen, Australia.

Smith, H. (1958) *The Religions of Man*, Harper & Brothers, New York.

Spencer, S. (1963) *Mysticism in World Religion*, Penguin, UK.

Van der Weyer, R. and Saunders, P. (1990) *The Creation Spirit (An Anthology)*, Darton, Longman & Todd, London.

Walker, K. (1942) *Diagnosis of Man*, Jonathan Cape, London.

Wilber, K. (1983) *Up from Eden*, Routledge & Kegan Paul, London.